To read any of Don Whitney's writings is to know the man as he truly is: extraordinarily disciplined, carefully precise, devoted to knowing Christ, and overflowing with joy in Christian fellowship. This collection of essays is a fitting tribute to a servant of Christ who has been such a rich blessing to Christians longing to grow in their devotion to God. The topics are varied, but all helpful. Each one will be of encouragement to the reader who wishes to grow in their knowledge of and delight in the Triune God.

—Matthew J. Hall, Provost, The Southern Baptist Theological Seminary

Reading this "celebration writing" (or *festschrift*) for Dr Don Whitney brings two thoughts to mind. The first is commonplace: "A man is known by the company he keeps." The second is biblical: "How good and pleasant it is when brothers dwell together in unity." Written by a variety of respected pastors and theologians, the book itself is brim-full of instruction and wisdom. But what gives these pages a celebratory air is the way the authors are so obviously united in their sense of brotherhood with, and personal appreciation for, Don Whitney and his work. The quality and interest of the essays, and the learning they represent, combine to honour someone whose friendship, teaching ministry, and books, have helped shape the lives of so many Christians today. *The Spirit of Holiness* is simply a wonderful expression of God's own promise: "Those who honour me I will honour."

—Sinclair B Ferguson, Chancellor's Professor of Systematic Theology, Reformed Theological Seminary

I am thankful for Terry Delany and the other contributors for putting together such an important work in honor of Don Whitney. I am even more thankful for Don Whitney, who for so many decades of faithful ministry has demonstrated a life and ministry worthy of praise. Read this book and be encouraged, practice this book and be spiritually enriched.

—Jason K. Allen, President of Midwestern Baptist Theological Seminary and Spurgeon College

These essays in honor of Donald Whitney genuinely do justice to him because they are insightful, biblical, engaging admonitions to pursue and imitate Christ. I cannot imagine a more stellar assortment of authors nor a more fitting subject matter in tribute to one who has consistently challenged us in the area of biblical spirituality. Each of these chapters, whether through history or theology, takes up that mantle and makes us yearn expectantly for the Holy Spirit to do His work in us.

—Hershael W. York, Dean, School of Theology, Victor & Louise Lester Professor of Preaching, The Southern Baptist Theological Seminary

THE SPIRIT
of
HOLINESS

REFLECTIONS
on
BIBLICAL SPIRITUALITY

THE SPIRIT
of
HOLINESS

REFLECTIONS
on
BIBLICAL SPIRITUALITY

Edited by

TERRY DELANEY

&

ROGER D. DUKE

LEXHAM PRESS

Print ISBN 9781683593249
Digital ISBN 9781683593256
Library of Congress Control Number 2020941133

Lexham Editorial: Todd Hains, Danielle Thevenaz, Abigail Stocker
Cover Design: George Siler
Typesetting: Sarah Vaughan

CONTENTS

PREFACE

Spirituality is a buzzword on the current church scene in North America. A plethora of books exist that one could read in order to be enlightened in the methods of becoming more "spiritual" but not necessarily more Christlike. Sadly, many of these methods are less about Christianity than about spirituality. From labyrinth walking to mind-emptying meditation, these methods recall that telling biblical text in Judges: "Everyone did what was right in his own eyes" (Judg 21:25b).

Since first publishing his work *Spiritual Disciplines for the Christian Life*, Donald S. Whitney has sought to redeem this field of spirituality—in some ways a menagerie!—by elucidating the classical spiritual disciplines. Instead of using any and every means one might be able to think of, Don instead has sought to limit the means of grace to the word of God. To that point, he has made fashionable the phrase "biblical spirituality" through his writings, his seminary-level courses at The Southern Baptist Theological Seminary, and his itinerant conference and preaching ministry in local churches.

In so doing, Don has managed to bring the academic study of spirituality to bear upon the daily lives of countless Christians through the ministry of the local church. Whereas many Christians look upon higher theological education as suspect, Don's academic writing offers a sweet balm to hurting souls who want to know how they can walk closer with the Lord. They want to do more than merely read their Bible; they want to become more like Christ, and they have come to realize that this will require discipline (Rom 12:2). But more often than not, they do not know where to begin. That is where Don's ministry has aided the most. He helps Christians to look to the word of God and seek to discipline themselves for the purpose of godliness. And at the very heart of all of this is Don's ultimate aim to glorify God.

Central to Don's ministry has always been the word of God. If a particular spiritual discipline is not found in the Bible, then it is, by default, not a biblical spiritual discipline. When he writes of various spiritual disciplines, he only writes of those that are found explicitly in Scripture. And when a discipline is found in the Bible, he reasons, it will be found throughout the history of the church. He has sought to learn from giants of the faith like David Brainerd (on journaling), Jonathan Edwards (on meditation), George Muller (on prayer), and Charles Spurgeon (on Bible reading), to name only four, who have modeled biblical spirituality. Don is compelled to learn from those who in the past sought spiritual counsel from the word of God and handed down a biblically informed tradition of spiritual disciplines.

Don's second major focus has been simplicity. A spiritual walk should never be so difficult that it is beyond the abilities of a child of God who has been redeemed by the blood of Jesus Christ. It is true that discipline requires a level of commitment sometimes beyond the reach of young children who have professed faith, but they can pray. They can read a Bible or have a Bible read to them. They can sing hymns and psalms and spiritual songs (Col 3:16). They can begin to cultivate methods of meditation so that they learn from an early age to bring every thought captive to the Lord (2 Cor 10:5).

The essays collected in *The Spirit of Holiness* have all been written in honor of this distinct ministry of Donald S. Whitney. The reader will find a set of essays that, first, articulate how specific saints from the halls of church history—the Puritans, Thomas Manton, Hercules Collins, Jonathan Edwards, Andrew Fuller, Thomas Steevens, American evangelicals during the Civil War, and C. H. Spurgeon—practiced the classical spiritual disciplines and how we can imitate their faith. R. Albert Mohler's essay provides a transition to the second set of essays, which are more practice-oriented: he shares how Don's book *Spiritual Disciplines for the Christian Life* helped him to recover a genuine Protestant spiritual discipline. In the second set of essays, the subjects of providence, sanctification, perseverance, and the local church as the locus of spirituality help the reader to see how spirituality applies to everyday life.

It was a distinct joy to work with each author, all of whom were delighted to contribute an essay for this volume. All of them cleared their schedules in order to make it happen in a timely manner. One writer exclaimed, "I would be glad to do this for my good friend, Don." It is our prayer that these essays, written in honor of our friend and mentor in spirituality, Dr. Donald S. Whitney, be received as gladly by you, the reader, as they were written by the writers. To God be the glory!

Terry Delaney
Roger D. Duke

ABBREVIATIONS

BQ	*Baptist Quarterly*
CL	Collins, Hercules. *Counsel for the Living, Occasioned from the Dead: Or, A Discourse on Job III. 17,18. Arising from the Deaths of Mr. Fran. Bampfield and Mr. Zach. Ralphson.* London: George Larkin, 1684.
CWTM	Manton, Thomas. *The Complete Works of Thomas Manton.* London: James Nisbet, 1870–75; repr., Birmingham: Solid Ground Christian Books, 2008.
FW	Edwards, Jonathan. *Freedom of the Will.* In *WJE* vol. 1.
JER	Smith, John E., Harry S. Stout, and Kenneth P. Minkema, eds. *A Jonathan Edwards Reader.* New Haven: Yale University Press, 1995.
MTP	Spurgeon, Charles. *Metropolitan Tabernacle Pulpit.* Pasadena, TX: Pilgrim, 1970–2006.
NPSP	Spurgeon, Charles. *New Park Street Pulpit.* Pasadena, TX: Pilgrim, 1970–2006.
SJE	Kimnach, Wilson H., Kenneth P. Minkema, and Douglas A. Sweeney. *Sermons of Jonathan Edwards.* New Haven: Yale University Press, 1999.
TD	Spurgeon, Charles. *The Treasury of David.* New York: Funk & Wagnalls, 1887.

VP   Collins, Hercules. *A Voice from the Prison. Or, Meditations on Revelations III.XI. Tending To the Establishment of Gods Little Flock, In an Hour of Temptation.* London, 1684.

WJE   Edwards, Jonathan. *The Works of Jonathan Edwards.* 26 vols. Edited by Perry Miller, John Smith, Harry Stout, Kenneth Minkema, et al. New Haven: Yale University Press, 1957–2008.

THE DOCTRINE OF THE TRINITY IN PURITAN DEVOTIONAL WRITINGS

JOE HARROD

Yet this hope is left unto forlorn men, that there is a way to heaven and happiness. ... A way that men may securely and safely walk in, a way in which Christ will guide the[m], God the father will keep them, and the Holy Ghost lead them by the hand, and direct them in all the passages thereof.

—*Nicholas Byfield*, The Marrow of the Oracles of God

INTRODUCTION

This paper began as a question: How did the Puritan clergy teach the laity under their pastoral care to think devotionally about the Trinity?[1] That the Puritans strove to articulate and defend the doctrine of the Trinity during the long seventeenth century is indisputable, as Joel Beeke and Mark Jones have outlined in their substantive overview of Puritan Trinitarian

---

1. I am indebted to the help of two research assistants, Colin McCulloch and Kenneth Trax, in locating and organizing many of the resources used in this article, which was originally presented at the 2016 annual meeting of the Evangelical Theological Society.

thought.[2] Significant treatises by equally significant mid- to late seventeenth-century Puritan writers include those of Francis Cheynell (1608–65), Stephen Charnock (1628–80), and John Owen (1616–83), among others.[3] The works these men produced are spiritually rich and demonstrate significant depth of theological engagement with Scripture, patristic theology, Reformed dogmatics, and contemporary theological debates. In this chapter, however, I want to focus on a different set of authors and a different type of literature, namely the "affectionate practical English writers" of Puritan devotional works.[4]

Seventeenth-century Europe saw the printing and sales of devotional manuals expand rapidly, and England was no exception. Religious handbooks for both clergy and laity flourished among both Catholics and Protestants.[5] In her important study of this literature, now nearly ninety years old, Helen White laments that her contemporary critics had largely ignored these devotional writings.[6] Writing almost six decades later, historian Richard Lovelace reiterated this lacuna.[7] While a select few works that Lovelace and

2. Joel R. Beeke and Mark Jones, *A Puritan Theology: Doctrine for Life* (Grand Rapids: Reformation Heritage Books, 2012), 85–100.

3. Francis Cheynell, *The Divine Triunity of the Father, Son, and Holy Spirit: or, The Blessed Doctrine of the three Coessentiall Subsistents in the eternall Godhead without any confusion or division of the distinct subsistences, or multiplication of the most single and entire Godhead, Acknowledged, believed, adored by Christians, in opposition to Pagans, Jewes, Mahumetaus, blasphemous and Antichristian Hereticks, who say they are Christians, but are not* (London, 1650); Cheynell, *The Rise, Growth, and Danger of Socinianisme* (London, 1643); Stephen Charnock, *Several Discourses upon the Existence and Attributes of God* (London, 1682); John Owen, *Communion with God*, in *The Works of John Owen*, ed. William H. Goold (repr., Edinburgh: Banner of Truth Trust, 1965), 2:5–274; Owen, *A Brief Declaration and Vindication of the Doctrine of the Trinity*, in Goold, *Works of John Owen*, 2:365–454.

4. The designation "affectionate practical English writers" is that of Richard Baxter, *A Christian Directory: or, a Summ of Practical Theologie, and Cases of Conscience* (London, 1673), 922. Baxter lists dozens of authors and works.

5. Charles E. Hambrick-Stowe, "Practical Divinity and Spirituality," in *The Cambridge Companion to Puritanism*, ed. John Coffey and Paul C. H. Lim (Cambridge: Cambridge University Press, 2008), 196.

6. Helen C. White, *English Devotional Literature: Prose 1600–1640*, University of Wisconsin Studies in Language and Literature 29 (New York: Haskell House, 1966), 9. White's work was originally compiled in 1930.

7. Richard Lovelace, "The Anatomy of Puritan Piety: English Puritan Devotional Literature, 1600–1640," in *Christian Spirituality: Post-Reformation and Modern*, vol. 18, *World Spirituality: An Encyclopedic History of the Religious Quest*, ed. Louis Dupré and Don E. Saliers (New York: Crossroad, 1989), 294–95.

White treated have been reproduced in the past quarter-century, the large body of these devotional writings remains largely neglected.[8]

PURITAN DEVOTIONAL WRITINGS

What features distinguish such devotional works from other Puritan literary efforts? Lovelace has noted the diversity of forms within this literature, including "manuals of godliness, manuals of comfort, spiritual treasuries, combat manuals, martyrologies, allegories, tracts, and prayer manuals."[9] According to White, regardless of its style,

> the book of devotion leaves all matter of controversy and of explanation and of interpretation to the defenders and the doctors of faith and concentrates its resources on the realization of that pattern of life which all religious effort strives to commend and to the exploration and the appropriation of those values which religion seeks to vindicate and propagate.[10]

Although White may have overstated her case regarding polemics and theology, she is right to emphasize the practical, experiential bent of this literature. With regard to their reception, Charles Hambrick-Stowe asserts that "these popular texts became a means by which Puritan practical divinity was translated into regular spiritual practices by individuals, families and devotional groups."[11]

J. I. Packer identifies learned Cambridge theologian William Perkins (1558–1602) as the father figure of the type of affective (affectionate) writing that flourished in seventeenth-century England.[12] Thomas Cooper, writing

---

8. Soli Deo Gloria books reprinted Lewis Bayly's *Practice of Piety*, and Reformation Heritage Books will release ten volumes of William Perkins's writings.

9. Lovelace, "Anatomy of Puritan Piety," 294.

10. White, *English Devotional Literature*, 12.

11. Hambrick-Stowe, "Practical Divinity and Spirituality," 196.

12. J. I. Packer, *A Quest for Godliness: The Puritan Vision of the Christian Life* (Wheaton, IL: Crossway, 1990), 50.

in 1609, commended the "many excellent Treatises and larger discourses, concerning the power of godlinesse" that had lately appeared in his own day, and a marginal note indicates that Perkins along with other Puritan fathers Richard Greenham (c. 1535–94), Richard Rogers (c. 1550–1618), John Downame (1571–1652), and Arthur Dent (d. 1607) were the authors of these works.[13] The decades that followed Cooper's commendation saw a steady stream of authors expand this body of literature.[14] These works vary in length and style from Henry Burton's relatively brief hundred-page prayer guide, *Triall of Private Devotions* (1628), to John Downame's nearly one thousand-page manual, *A Guide to Godlynesse* (1622). Given the experiential emphasis of these works, the doctrine of sanctification is the unifying theme, and discussion of specific practices such as prayer, meditation, the ordinances, and the like abound. What can such devotional writings teach us about how Puritan pastors wed theology and piety, specifically with regard to the Trinity? In the remainder of this paper I answer this question by considering the Trinitarian reflections of several devotional works and how authors of such works connected the doctrine of the Trinity to the practice of prayer.

LEWIS BAYLY, *THE PRACTICE OF PIETY* (C. 1612)

Among early seventeenth-century devotional writers, few had as wide-ranging or lingering an influence as did Lewis Bayly (c. 1575–1631), whose *The Practice of Piety* was one of the most popular devotional guides of its day

---

13. Thomas Cooper, *The Christian's Daily Sacrifice: Containing a daily Direction for a Setled course of Sanctification* (London, 1609), A5. I am indebted to Lovelace, "Anatomy of Puritan Piety," 294, for the reference.

14. The following list is representative, not exhaustive, and builds on the work of Lovelace: Robert Allwyn, *The Oyle of Gladnesse: or, Musicke at the House of Mourning* (London, 1631); William Attersoll, *Three Treatises* (London, 1632); John Ball, *The Power of Godlines* (London, 1657); Lewis Bayly, *The Practice of Pietie* (London, 1616); Paul Baynes, *Briefe Directions unto a Godly Life* (London, 1637); Robert Bolton, *Some Generall Directions for a Comfortable Walking with God* (London, 1626); Richard Brathwaite, *A Spiritual Spicerie* (London, 1638); Nicholas Byfield, *The Marrow of the Oracles of God* (London, 1630); John Dod, *The Bright Star Which Leadeth Wise Men to Our Lord Jesus Christ* (London, 1603); John Downame, *A Guide to Godlynesse* (London, 1622); Downame, *The Christian Warfare* (London, 1604); Daniel Featley, *Ancilla Pietatis, or The Handmaid to Private Devotion* (London, 1626); Phineas Fletcher, *Joy in Tribulation* (London, 1632); Samuel Hieron, *A Helpe unto Devotion*, 4th ed. (London, 1612); Thomas Howes, *Markes of Salvation* (London, 1637); William Pulley, *The Christian's Task* (London, 1619); Henry Scudder, *A Key of Heaven* (London, 1632); Edward Vaughn, *A Plaine and Perfect Method, for the Easy Understanding of the Whole Bible* (London, 1617).

and thus merits a fuller discussion here.[15] Bayly was of Welsh ancestry and was educated at Oxford, where he took a bachelor of divinity in 1611 and a doctor of divinity in 1613. During his early ministry, in the first decade of the 1600s, he preached sermons that became the substance of *The Practice of Piety*, the earliest extant edition of the book being the second, published in 1612. The book was richly footnoted, showing Bayly's depth of theological reading and engagement.[16] Bayly went to London as rector of St. Matthew's, Friday Street, and was appointed as chaplain to Prince Henry of Wales, to whom he dedicated *Practice*. In 1616 Bayly became chaplain to King James I (1566–1625), who appointed him as bishop of Bangor, in north Wales. Though Bayly remained loyal to church authority, his theology and spirituality were from the Puritan mold. In 1621 Bayly's Puritan sympathies led to a brief imprisonment for opposing the Book of Sports. Nine years later he defended himself against charges of ordaining clergy disloyal to Anglican order. Bayly died in 1631, his enduring legacy preserved in the pages of his devotional manual.[17]

The Practice of Piety was widely received. Fifty-nine editions appeared between 1611 and 1735, with dozens more following through the nineteenth century. During Bayly's lifetime it was translated into Welsh, French, and German. In the decades that followed, the work spread east to Poland and west to Massachusetts, where missionary John Eliot rendered it into the language of Christian Native Americans.[18] As was common for such literature, the work was especially popular among the poor, a fact illustrated

---

15. Anthony Milton, "Puritanism and the Continental Reformed Churches," in Coffey and Lim, *Cambridge Companion to Puritanism*, 117. Bayly is at times printed as Bailie.

16. Just within the first chapter Bayly cites Athanasius, Basil, Chrysostom, Gregory of Nazianzus, Augustine, Irenaeus, Aquinas, Bucer, Melancthon, Gabriel Biel, and Thomas à Kempis, among others.

17. This biographical sketch is drawn from Joel R. Beeke and Randall J. Pedersen, *Meet the Puritans* (Grand Rapids: Reformation Heritage Books, 2006), 72–74. See also T. F. Tout, "Bayly, Lewis (d. 1631)," in *The Dictionary of National Biography*, ed. Leslie Stephen (New York: Macmillan, 1885), 3:448–49.

18. Eliot's abridgment and translation is titled *Manitowompae Pomantamoonk* (1665). On the spread of *The Practice of Piety*, see Milton, "Puritanism and the Continental Reformed Churches," 117.

most famously by the testimony of the Baptist pastor and allegorist John Bunyan (1628–88).[19]

The Practice of Piety presents a comprehensive view of Christian spiritual practice.[20] It opens with "A Plain Description of the Essence and Attributes of God."[21] Beginning with this theology proper, Bayly provides a series of meditations in which he contrasts the miseries of those estranged from God with the blessedness of those who are reconciled through Christ. The fourth chapter examines common hindrances to the practice of piety. In subsequent chapters Bayly provides sample meditations to guide believers in morning and evening prayers, prayers to be used to promote piety within one's household, directions for singing the Psalter, for reading Scripture, and for pursuing daily fellowship with God, and a series of meditations and prayers for the rhythm of the church calendar, for the key events of life, and for when one is facing death. Four such meditations guide believers to the Supper.

KNOWLEDGE OF GOD AS TRINITY

Jones and Beeke remind us that a twofold approach to the doctrine of God typifies theology proper, that is, approaches tend to consider God either by essence or person.[22] In around thirty pages of tightly argued material, Bayly adopts both approaches. In keeping with the Reformed tradition, Bayly asserts that true Christian piety consists in knowing "the essence of God" and "thy owne selfe."[23] With regard to oneself, one must give attention to

---

19. In Bunyan's autobiography, *Grace Abounding to the Chief of Sinners* (1666), the Bedford pastor recounts the slender means that he and his first wife suffered, yet his wife brought a far richer dowry to their marriage than either realized at the time: two books given by her godly father, Dent's *The Plain Man's Pathway to Heaven* (1601) and Bayly's *Practice of Piety*. It was through these books that Bunyan's conscience was first stirred toward Christianity. See John Bunyan, *Grace Abounding to the Chief of Sinners*, ed. W. R. Owens (London, Penguin Books, 1987), 9–10.

20. Hambrick-Stowe, "Practical Divinity and Spirituality," 197.

21. Lewis Bayly, *The Practice of Piety: Directing a Christian how to walk, that he may please God*, 53rd ed., corrected (London, Three Crowns, 1719), 4. In the analysis that follows Bayly's spelling and capitalization are retained, but words appearing in italics in the original have not been italicized herein.

22. Joel R. Beeke and Mark Jones, *A Puritan Theology: Doctrine for life* (Grand Rapids: Reformation Heritage Books, 2012), 85.

23. This idea is found in John Calvin's *Institutes of the Christian Religion*, book 1, chapter 1. Bayly, however, cites Martin Bucer on this point.

both one's corruption and renovation. With respect to God, the pious must understand "the divers manner of being therein, which are Three Persons" and "the Attributes thereof." Bayly's thesis is that "the knowledge of God's majesty, and man's misery" form the "first and chiefest grounds of the practice of piety." Such knowledge precedes true devotion: "Unless that a man doth truly know God, he neither can, nor will worship him aright: for how can a man love him, whom he knoweth not? And who will worship him, whose help a man thinks he needed not?" Even the first chapter's heading expresses the priority of theological knowledge: "A Plaine description of the Essence and Attributes of God, out of the holy Scripture, so farre forth as every Christian must competently know, and necessarily believe, that will be saved." Citing a catena of biblical texts, Bayly summarizes God's essence succinctly: "God is that one, spiritual, and infinitely perfect Essence, whose Being is of himself eternally."[24]

God is one substance and three persons; not three substances but rather three subsistences. The three persons of the Godhead may be distinguished in name, order, and actions. In name the persons are Father, Son, and Holy Spirit. The Father is so named because of his relation to Christ and to his children adopted by grace. The Son is identified as such because he is begotten eternally of his Father's substance. The Holy Spirit is incorporeal and "breathed from both the Father and the Son." With regard to order, "The Father is the First Person in the glorious Trinity, having neither his Being nor Beginning of any other but of himself; begetting his Son, and together with his Son sending forth the Holy Ghost from everlasting."[25] Bayly notes two sorts of distinguishing works: internal works respecting the Godhead and external works respecting the world. Externally, God creates, redeems, and sanctifies. Internally God begets, is begotten, and proceeds.[26] For the sake of time I will omit further elaboration of Bayly's discussion of God's

24. Bayly, *Practice of Piety*, 2–4. Bayly cites Ps 143:3; 1 Tim 6:16; Deut 1:4; 4:35; 6:4; 32:39; Isa 45:5–8; 1 Cor 8:4; Eph 4:5–6; 1 Tim 2:5; John 4:24; 2 Cor 3:17; 1 Kgs 8:17; Ps 147:5; Deut 32:4; and Exod 3:14 to support his definition.

25. Bayly, *Practice of Piety*, 5–7.

26. Bayly uses Nicaean language with regard to the passive "action" of the Son being begotten: "This [action] belongeth only to the Son, who is of the Father alone, not made, nor created, but begotten" (*Practice of Piety*, 12).

names and attributes. Bayly's opening comments are striking. First, they give
priority to a theology of God grounded on biblical revelation. Then, they
require both faith and understanding as requisite for salvation. Not only are
piety and knowledge intertwined; they are inseparable.

John Downame, in his massive *Guide to Godlynesse* (1622), echoes Bayly's
emphasis on the necessity of knowing God. Human understanding of God
essence is impossible (no creature can fully comprehend its Creator):

> But who he is, he hath made known in his Word; namely,
> that he is *Jehovah Elohim*, a Spirit infinite in all perfection, one
> in nature, and three in persons, the Father, Son and Holy
> Ghost. By which description it appeareth, that God is *primum
> est*, and the first being, who hath his essence of himself, and
> giveth being to all things, as his name Jehovah signifieth; that
> he is uncreated, and the Spirit, as our Savior, the wisdom
> of the Father, hath made him known unto us, not so much
> thereby shewing his essence what he is, which is ineffable and
> incomprehensible, as distinguishing him from all corporeal
> substances.[27]

Christians must seek to know God according to his self-revelation as Trinity:
"A person in the deity is a subsistence in the divine essence, comprehending
the whole divine nature and essence in it, but distinguished by an
incommunicable property from other persons, unto which it hath relation."
While the persons within the Godhead remain distinct, each person is united
in action: "Whatsoever agreeth absolutely to, or is spoken of the whole divine
nature, in respect of its outward actions and works toward the creatures, doth
alike agree to every distinct person, and whatsoever agreeth to, or is spoken
of every of the persons, that likewise agreeth to the whole divine nature."[28]

---

27. Downame, *Guide to Godlynesse*, 30.
28. Downame, *Guide to Godlynesse*, 33–34.

William Attersoll (d. 1640), sometimes minister at Isfield in Sussex, instructed readers of his *Three Treatises* on the personal and essential distinctions within the Godhead:

> Now touching the meaning, this word (Father) so far as it is ascribed to God, is taken sometimes personally, and sometimes essentially. Personally, when it is restrained to one of the Persons, as to the first Person in the holy and blessed Trinity to wit, God the Father begetting the Son, and sending forth the Holy Ghost, whensoever mention is made of any of the other Persons also. Thus likewise it is taken, when it is limited to the second Person in Trinity, to wit, God the Son, begotten of the Father before all worlds. … And in this sense, the Holy Ghost the third Person proceeding from the Father and the Son, may also be called Father, because he together with the Father and the Son giveth being to all things.[29]

The title "Father" might also be used essentially, without reference to personal distinctions or relations, especially as it relates to the church:

> The Father, the Son, and the Holy Ghost, who have a sovereign Father-hood over the Church, loving it, defending it, delighting in it, caring for it, bestowing all blessings upon it, and withholding nothing that is good from it. This title teaches us, that God is the Father of his Church and Children. As a Father loveth his Children, to whom he hath given breath and being, as he feedeth and clotheth them, nourisheth and layeth up for them: so God loveth his Children to whom he

---

29. Attersoll, *Three Treatises*, 92–93. The three treatises are (1) "The Conversion of Nineveh"; (2) "God's Trumpet Sounding the Alarum"; and (3) "Physicke against Famine." These treatises are sermons expanded for publication. In "Nineveh," Attersoll considers the practices of fasting and prayer as well as confession and repentance. In "God's Trumpet" Attersoll urges the "practice of true repentance" (A1). In "Physicke," Attersoll explains God's nature as shepherd of his church.

hath given their first life, their Second Life and to whom he
will give a third life.[30]

Even in their practical exhortations on the mechanics of sanctification,
Puritan devotional authors rarely shied away from declaring deep and
intricate doctrine. Some statements are brief, even when found in unexpected
places, such as John Dod's mention of the sanctifying work of the Trinity,
which occurs in his exposition of the Decalogue:

> If God have regenerated us and Christ have killed our sins, &
> the Holy Ghost make us ashamed of them, & confess them
> and it work in us Love & Patience and moderation of our
> affections, and make us able to pray unto God, then God is
> our God, and then this will make us obey.[31]

Other mentions, such as those by Bayly and Downame, are more complex.
Yet such authors could insist that lay readers must know and understand
nuanced concepts such as the Son's eternal generation or the double
procession of the Spirit. They expected readers to comprehend personal
and essential distinctions and to appreciate the inseparable or indivisible
works of the Trinity. One area where Trinitarian doctrine and pious living
meet is in Puritan works on prayer.

THE TRINITY AND PRAYER

Puritan devotional writings may have different foci, but rare is the manual
that ignores the topic of prayer. Simply surveying the vast devotional
literature on this subject would require a study unto itself, yet for our purpose
a sampling will let us see how often these devotional writings discuss the
doctrine of the Trinity in relation to the task of prayer, especially the Lord's
Prayer.

---

30. Attersoll, *Three Treatises*, 92–93.
31. John Dod, *The Bright Star which Leadeth Wise men to our Lord Jesus Christ* (London, 1603), 12.

Though Henry Scudder is perhaps better known for his *Christian's Daily Walk*, a work that in later reprints featured prefatory advertisements from Baxter and Owen attesting its benefits, Scudder's *Key of Heaven* "opens and applies" the Lord's Prayer to teach Christians how to pray.[32] Yet even in such practical exposition, Scudder finds occasion to teach Trinitarian dogma as he explains the use of the title "Father" in the prayer:

> Father, spoken of God is a word of relation to Christ the second person in Trinity, and so is proper to the first person in Trinity: Secondly, in relation to the creature, in a more common respect to all, as he is the Author of their being, and subsisting in nature; thus all three persons are called Father. God is also a Father in a special respect to his elect in Christ, as he is the Author of their spiritual being and subsisting in state of grace. Thus in special sort the three persons are, and may be called Father by all beleevers. And, as I conceive, in this place this word Father directeth us to God the Father, God the Son, and God the Holy Ghost; yet so as it pointeth, in an order, to that person in the Deity to whom Fatherhood, and the beginning of all things is ascribed, without excluding, but necessarily including the other two; namely, to God the Father, the first person in Trinity, the natural and eternal Father of Christ Jesus; who by adopting us in Christ, and by begetting us again by regeneration through the Spirit is our Father.[33]

Scudder's teaching seems consistent with that of William Perkins's *Exposition of the Lord's Prayer* (1593), which poses several questions in Perkins's exposition of the prayer, including "Whether wee are to praye to the Sonne and holye Ghost as to the Father."

---

32. Scudder, *Key of Heaven*, title page.
33. Scudder, *Key of Heaven*, 89–90.

Perkins answers affirmatively: "Invocation belonges to all the three persons in Trinitie; and not onely to the Father," for passages such as Acts 7:59; 1 Thessalonians 3:2; and 2 Corinthians 13:13 show believers praying to each divine personage, and while "father sonne and holie ghost are three distinct persons, yet they are not to be severed or divided; because they all subsiste in one and the same Godhead or divine nature." Neither are the persons of the Trinity divided in their work: "In all outward actions, as in the creation and preservation of the world, and the salvation of the elect, they are not severed or divided; for they all worke together, onlie they are distinguished in the manner of working." Knowledge of the Trinity is essential for genuine prayer: "This [knowledge] being the lowest and firste foundation of praier, it is requisite that all of which would pray or write, should have this knowledge rightly to believe of the Trinitie, and to know howe the three persons agree and howe they are distinguished."[34]

In a similar manner, John Ball (1585–1640) uses a question-answer rhetoric to instruct believers in prayer:

> Q. Our Saviour teacheth us to pray, Our Father: must we not then pray to the Son, and the holy Spirit?

> A. As we are baptized into the Name of the Father, Son, and Holy Ghost, so are we to call upon the Father, Son, and Holy Ghost: for they are one in essence, the object of religious adoration, and stand in such natural relation to each other, that when one is invocated, all are invocated.[35]

Practically, believers cannot avoid conceptualizing the Trinity as they pray, for "every act of religion doth require that we some way apprehend the object of it; and as there can be no site without some visible object propounded: so no act of religious worship without this object in some wise

---

34. William Perkins, *An exposition of the Lord's prayer: in the way of catechizing serving for ignorant people* (London, 1593), 29–30, 32.

35. John Ball, *Power of Godlines*, 362.

conceived."[36] Believers are free to invoke God generally, or any individual member particularly, but drawing on the doctrine of the Trinity's indivisible works, Ball states,

> It is lawful also when we name persons, to name one only, two, or all the three, provided that we name not one as excluding the other two, nor yet to as excluding the third; for thus calling on one, we invoke all: and as naming no person distinctly, we do not dishonor the persons: so naming one and not others, doth not breed any inquality of honour in our worship.[37]

CONCLUSION

This chapter has provided a brief introduction to the devotional writings of the seventeenth-century Puritans with attention to how various authors in different works used this genre as a vehicle for teaching the doctrine of the Trinity to the laity. A fuller treatment would incorporate other sorts of writings such as sermons, catechisms, journals, autobiographies, and personal letters, for such items would add more intimate dimension to this study. Yet even with its restrictions, our study yields several conclusions.

First, contrary to White's assessment, seventeenth-century Puritan devotional works hardly leave matters of polemics or teaching to the side, but rather ground their practical conclusions in such teaching. This approach emphasizes the coinherence of theology and piety. Doctrine was not a matter to be relegated to trained clergy, but a vital aspect of sanctification for all the faithful. Second, although none of the devotional writings reviewed were works written for the explicit purpose of explaining the Trinity, many authors included extended and detailed Trinitarian teaching, indicating that for these pastor-theologians, right understanding of the person of God was essential for living Christianly.

36. Ball, *Power of Godlines*, 362.
37. Ball, *Power of Godlines*, 362.

Perhaps the best way to conclude an examination of Puritan Trinitarian devotion is with a prayer composed for the devout layperson facing death:

> Glorious Creator, gracious Redeemer, everlasting comforter, Lord God Almightly,
>
> Send me ayde and help from heaven in this my last and most dreadful conflict with all the powers of hell and darknesse.
>
> Arme mee with thy compleat armour, and endue me with power from above to vanquish Sathan and his infernal bands, and to quench all the fiere darts of the wicked in the blood of my Redeemer.
>
> I am thine, O God the Father, by the right of creation;
>
> I am thine, O God the Son, by the right of thy purchase;
>
> I am thine, O God the holy Ghost, by the right of thine inhabitation, and possession.
>
> Save mee, Father, by thy power;
>
> Save mee, Sonne, by thy merits;
>
> Save mee, holy Spirit, by the grace.
>
> O holy, blessed and glorious Trinity,
>
> Whose power no creature is able to resist:
>
> Rebuke and confound thine enemy that goeth about to deface thine image in Mee;
>
> To spoile thy workmanship;
>
> To destroy him for whom thou, o Son, offeredst thy selfe on the crosse by the eternal Spirit to the Father.
>
> Into thy hands, O Father, who breathedst into mee the spirit of life;
>
> Into thy hands, O Sonne, who breathedest out thy Spirit for mee;
>
> Into thy hands, O Holy Spirit, who renewedst a right spirit within me, and hast comforted my spirit to the last gaspe,
>
> I now commend my Spirit,
>
> Amen.[38]

---

38. Daniel Featley, *Ancilla Pietatis*, 707–10.

THE GREAT FUEL OF FAITH

Meditation in the Piety of Thomas Manton

STEPHEN YUILLE

What are we to God? Do we have any effect on him? Does he gain anything from us? Does he need us? "Can a man be profitable to God?" (Job 22:2).[1] For Thomas Manton, the answer is a resounding *no*. We cannot add anything to an all-sufficient God who is fully and completely satisfied in himself. Manton views this as a positive thing, because only an all-sufficient God is able to satisfy us. He states, "Though God stand in no need of us, yet he is willing to communicate his blessedness, and to make us happy in the enjoyment of himself."[2] For Manton, God does so by impressing His goodness upon us. As it comes into focus, we experience "the well-pleasedness of the soul in God as an all-sufficient portion."[3] This "well-pleasedness" then increases our *faith*, which, in turn, is the root of all *graces* such as love, hope, patience, and zeal, and the root of all *effects* such as spiritual sense, strength, and affection.[4]

According to Manton, this impression of God's goodness on us and our experience of "well-pleasedness" (the root of faith and, thus, all graces and effects) constitutes the essence of the spiritual life. At the foundation of this

---

1. All Scripture quotations in this chapter are from the ESV.
2. Thomas Manton, *Psalm 119*, CWTM 6:111.
3. Thomas Manton, *Sermons on Romans 8*, CWTM 12:278.
4. Thomas Manton, *Life of Faith*, CWTM 15:48, 50–53.

life stands God's word. The reason is obvious: all spiritual graces and effects flow from faith; faith flows from an apprehension of God's goodness; and an apprehension of God's goodness is "fed and increased" by God's word.[5] Because there can be no faith without God's word, Manton is adamant that we must "busy ourselves" with it through the use of spiritual duties such as reading, hearing, meditating, praying, singing, using the seals, and keeping the Sabbath.[6] Among these duties meditation emerges as the most important because it enlivens all the others, thereby making them "fruitful to our souls."[7] This means that, in terms of the spiritual life, meditation is "the great fuel of faith"—the chief means by which faith is "begotten" and "increased."[8]

The purpose of this chapter is to consider this critical component of Manton's biblical piety.

5. Based on Rom 10:14–15, Manton affirms that God's word is the means to "beget and breed" faith. Thomas Manton, *Sermons on 2 Thessalonians 1:3*, *CWTM* 17:126.

6. Thomas Manton, *Life of Faith*, 55, 163. Also see *Sermons on Matthew 25*, *CWTM* 9:345–46, 396; *Sermons on John 17*, *CWTM* 10:144–45; 11:12–14; *Sermons on Titus 2:11–14*, *CWTM* 16:155–60. If faith comes by hearing the word, then how can faith be necessary to make the word effectual? Manton explains, "At first God by his preventing grace taketh hold of the heart, and maketh it to believe; as at the first creation light was made before the sun; and the first man was made out of the dust of the ground, afterwards he propagateth and bringeth forth after his kind; so that the first work might be exempted from the common rule, yet not the subsequent works" (*Life of Faith*, 15:170). Lewis Bayly maintains that the essence of piety is "to join together, in watching, fasting, praying, reading the Scriptures, keeping his Sabbaths, hearing sermons, receiving the holy Communion, relieving the poor, exercising in all humility the works of piety to God, and walking conscionably in the duties of our calling towards men." See Bayly, *The Practice of Piety*, 163. According to E. Glenn Hinson, this statement sums up "the whole Puritan platform." See Hinson, "Puritan Spirituality," in *Protestant Spiritual Traditions*, ed. F. C. Senn (New York: Paulist Press, 1986), 165.

7. Manton, *Psalm 119*, 7:479. Manton rebukes those who minimize the importance of meditation: "Young and green heads look upon meditation as a dull melancholy work, fit only for the phlegm and decay of old age; vigorous and eager spirits are more for action than thoughts, and their work lieth so much with other that they have no time to descend into themselves." See Thomas Manton, *Sermons on Genesis 24:63*, *CWTM* 17:264. He is so convinced of its importance that he warns: "The beast under the law that did not chew the cud was unclean." See Thomas Manton, *Exposition of James*, *CWTM* 4:160.

8. Thomas Manton, *Sermons on Hebrews 11*, *CWTM* 13:376–77. The subject of meditation appears repeatedly throughout Manton's collected works. His most extensive treatment is found in *Sermons on Genesis 24:63*, 263–350.

LIFE AND MINISTRY

Thomas Manton was born at Lydeard St. Lawrence, Somerset, on March 31, 1620.[9] After completing grammar school, he enrolled at Wadham College, Oxford, and graduated four years later with a bachelor of arts. Since advanced degrees did not require his presence at Oxford, he went on to complete the bachelor of divinity in 1654 and the doctor of divinity in 1660 while engaged in ministry. Upon his ordination to the diaconate in 1639, Manton embarked on his first lectureship at the parish church of Culliton (Colyton), Devon. In order to avoid the growing political unrest in the region, he moved a short time later with his new bride, Mary Morgan, to London. In 1644, St. Mary's Stoke Newington was sequestered, and the pastorate was offered to Manton. He held this position until becoming pastor of St. Paul's Covent Garden a few years later.

These were eventful years for the nation, and Manton found himself in the midst of significant social and political upheaval. While it is true that he served as one of the three clerks at the Westminster Assembly, penned the introduction to the documents of the Westminster Assembly, preached occasionally before Parliament, and prayed at various ceremonies related to Oliver Cromwell's protectorship, Manton remained a committed royalist. He was one of fifty-seven divines who signed a protest against Parliament's plan to execute the king.

Despite his outspoken opposition to the regicide, Manton was a prominent figure during Oliver Cromwell's protectorship. He became a leading voice in

9. The standard account of Manton's life is William Harris, "Some Memoirs of the Life and Character of the Reverend and Learned Thomas Manton, D.D.," *CWTM* 1:vii–xxxiii. Harris's biographical sketch is based on two earlier accounts: William Bates, "A Funeral Sermon Preached upon the Death of the Reverend and Excellent Divine, Dr. Thomas Manton," *CWTM* 22:123–47; and Anthony Wood, *Athenae Oxonienses* (London, 1691), 2:446–48. Additional summaries of Manton's life are found in Edmund Calamy, *The Nonconformist's Memorial: Being an account of the ministers, who were ejected or silenced after the Restoration, particularly by the Act of Uniformity, which took place on Bartholomew-day, Aug. 24, 1662* (London, 1775), 1:138–41; and Joel R. Beeke and Randall J. Pederson, *Meet the Puritans: With a Guide to Modern Reprints* (Grand Rapids: Reformation Heritage Books, 2006), 407–9. For a more thorough analysis of Manton in his historical context, see Derek Cooper, "The Ecumenical Exegete: Thomas Manton's Commentary on James in Relation to Its Protestant Predecessors, Contemporaries and Successors" (PhD diss., Lutheran Theological Seminary, 2008); and Adam Richardson, "Thomas Manton and the Presbyterians in Interregnum and Restoration England" (PhD diss., University of Leicester, 2014).

political and theological matters, serving on numerous commissions. After Richard Cromwell's protectorship failed in 1660, Manton was very active among those favorable to the return of Charles II. According to J. C. Ryle, "If there was one name which more than another was incessantly before the public for several years about the period of the Restoration, that name was Manton's."[10] He even served as one of the delegates who met with Charles II at Breda, in order to negotiate the terms of his return.

Upon his restoration, the king quickly swept away any hopes for compromise between Presbyterians and Episcopalians. His new parliament passed the Act of Uniformity in 1662, requiring all who had not received Episcopal ordination to be reordained by bishops; moreover, it required ministers to declare their consent to the entire Book of Common Prayer and their rejection of the Solemn League and Covenant. As a result, approximately two thousand ministers (including Manton) left the Church of England. While actively seeking accommodation for Presbyterians within the national church, Manton continued to preach privately. Because of his violation of the Five Mile Act, he was imprisoned for six months in 1670;[11] however, political indulgence two years later allowed him to preach openly at his home in Covent Garden. Soon after, he became a lecturer at Pinner's Hall and remained in this capacity until his death on October 18, 1677.

At Manton's funeral, William Bates preached on 1 Thessalonians 4:17, "And so shall we ever be with the Lord." In the course of his sermon, he praised his close friend for "the holiness of his person," extoling in particular his "constancy," "loyalty," "charity," and "humility." Bates also praised Manton for "the quality of his office," affirming that he possessed "a clear judgment, rich fancy, strong memory, and happy elocution."[12] These "parts," coupled with his extraordinary knowledge of Scripture, made him an excellent minister of the gospel. According to Bates, the goal of Manton's preaching was to open eyes so that people might see "their wretched condition as

---

10. J. C. Ryle, "An Estimate of Manton," *CWTM* 2:vii.

11. This act prohibited ministers from coming within five miles of the parish church from which they had been ejected.

12. Bates, "Funeral Sermon," 123–47. Ryle provides an insightful assessment of Manton as a "man," "writer," "theologian," and "expositor." See his "Estimate of Manton," iii–xiii.

sinners"; to cause them to flee "from the wrath to come"; to make them "humbly, thankfully and entirely" receive Christ as their all-sufficient Savior; and to edify them "in their most holy faith."[13] By all accounts, Bates's high estimation of Manton's preaching was fully warranted.[14] According to Edmund Calamy, Manton "left behind him the general reputation of as excellent a preacher as this city or nation hath produced."[15] He was a skilled spiritual physician who excelled at expounding and applying God's truth to those under his pastoral care.[16]

Over the course of his ministry, Manton preached numerous miscellaneous sermons, plus extensive series on the Lord's Prayer, Christ's temptation, Christ's transfiguration, Isaiah 53, 2 Thessalonians 2, Matthew 25, John 17, Romans 6 and 8, 2 Corinthians 5, Hebrews 11, Psalm 119, James, and Jude.[17] These sermons confirm his vision of the spiritual life—in sum, we rest in God as an all-sufficient portion as he impresses his goodness on us, and the resulting faith births all spiritual graces (e.g., love, hope, and patience) and effects (e.g., sense, strength, and affection). These sermons

---

13. Bates, "Funeral Sermon," 144. Manton was Reformed in his soteriology. See *CWTM* 3:328–31; 5:475–84; 12:295–96, 314–15; 20:326, 361. However, he modeled his preaching on Christ, particularly his free offer of the gospel. See *CWTM* 13:293. For a brief discussion of the relationship between his soteriology and preaching, see Donald J. MacLean, "Thomas Manton (1620–1677)," in *James Durham (1622–1658) and the Gospel Offer in Its Seventeenth-Century Context* (Göttingen: Vandenhoeck & Ruprecht, 2015), 197–214.

14. In the opinion of Archbishop James Ussher, Manton was one of the "best preachers in England" (cited in Harris, "Some Memoirs," xi).

15. Edmund Calamy, *An Abridgement of Mr. Baxter's History of His Life and Times* (London, 1702), 210.

16. Manton remarks, "Were we only to provide for ourselves, we might read to you fair lectures of contemplative divinity, and with words as soft as oil entice you into a fool's paradise, never searching your wounds and sores. But our commission is to 'cry aloud, and spare not' (Isaiah 58:1)" (*Exposition of James*, 436).

17. Manton's published works include close to one thousand sermons gathered into twenty-two volumes. Interestingly, they do not contain a single polemical or doctrinal treatise. All of his writings, therefore, are expositional. In the opinion of Hughes Oliphant Old, Manton's published works "probably give us the best sustained impression of Puritan preaching which is available." See *The Reading and Preaching of the Scriptures in the Worship of the Christian Church* (Grand Rapids: Eerdmans, 2002), 4:301. For an analysis of Manton as a biblical interpreter, see Derek Cooper, *Thomas Manton: A Guided Tour of the Life and Thought of a Puritan Pastor* (Phillipsburg, NJ: P&R, 2011), 79–142. Cooper's study focuses on Manton's sermons on the book of James.

also confirm that, for Manton, this *life* is chiefly maintained and cultivated by means of meditation on God's word.

THE PURPOSE OF MEDITATION

"If you mean to keep in the fire," writes Manton, "you must ply the bellows and blow hard."[18] His point is that meditation is the means by which we "blow hard" on our hearts, thereby igniting and enflaming love for God. As such, it involves far more than merely reading and hearing Scripture,[19] actions that are like "a winter sun that shineth, but warmeth not."[20] Meditation entails a serious "pondering" of God's word whereby its truths penetrate and capture the "very heart."[21]

This "pondering" is sometimes "occasional." Over the course of the day, we "spiritualize" those objects with which we are conversant, meaning we draw lessons from what we see of God's wonders in creation and providence. While this is a valuable exercise, Manton places far greater emphasis on "set and solemn" meditation, which he defines as "that duty and exercise of religion whereby the mind is applied to the serious and solemn consideration and improvement of the truths which we understand and believe, for practical uses and purposes."[22] It includes "observation," whereby we compare God's providence with his word, taking note of how he fulfills his promises and threats in his governance of human affairs. It also includes

---

18. Manton, *Psalm 119*, 7:80.

19. Manton, *Psalm 119*, 6:105–6.

20. Manton, *Psalm 119*, 6:140. Manton adds, "Reading and hearing are effectual by meditation" (*Psalm 119*, 9:80). Again, "The heart is hard and the memory slippery, the thoughts loose and vain; and therefore, unless we cover the good seed, the fowls of the air will catch it away" (*Psalm 119*, 6:141).

21. Manton, *Psalm 119*, 6:106. Manton adds, "We taste things better when they are chewed than when they are swallowed whole" (*Psalm 119*, 9:80).

22. Manton, *Psalm 119*, 6:139–40. Also see *Psalm 119*, 7:79. Manton identifies three kinds of "solemn and set" meditation. The first is "reflexive": "a solemn parlay between a man and his own heart (Ps. 4:4)." We function as our own "accuser" and "judge" as we examine our lives in the light of Scripture. The second is "dogmatical": "when we exercise ourselves in the doctrines of the word, and consider how truths known may be useful to us." The third is "practical": "when we take ourselves aside from worldly distractions, that we may solemnly debate and study how to carry on the holy life with better success and advantage" (*Sermons on Genesis 24:63*, 268–69).

"study and search," whereby we inquire into God's word to discover his will for us. Most importantly, however, it includes "consideration," whereby we ponder what we read and hear, determining what it means for our present "use and practice" and our eternal "weal or woe." When we meditate in this way, the truths of God's word work "upon the heart."[23]

This kind of meditation is on full display throughout Manton's works. A typical example is found in his exposition of Psalm 119:89–91, "Forever, O LORD, your word is firmly fixed in the heavens. Your faithfulness endures to all generations; you have established the earth, and it stands fast. By your appointment they stand this day, for all things are your servants." Based on these verses, Manton muses on the fact that God is "without beginning or ending," and that we are "enclosed between infiniteness before and infiniteness behind." As far as he is concerned, this truth "is not seriously and sufficiently enough thought of and improved, till it lessen all other things in our opinion and estimation of them and affection to them."[24] There is nothing that promotes "the great ends of the gospel" as much as meditation on God's eternality.

Manton works this truth on the heart by drawing out its practical implications. First, it makes Christ "precious" by exalting him as the only one who can deliver us from the wrath to come while procuring for us the eternal enjoyment of God. Second, it promotes "change" because it points to our smallness, thereby making "a proud man humble, a vain man serious, a covetous man heavenly, [and] a wicked man good." Third, it checks "temptations" by demonstrating that the pleasures, riches, and honors of this world are but "transitory things." Fourth, it quickens diligence because it reminds us of the importance of living in light of eternity. All told, it reminds us that the enjoyment of the eternal God is our "end and scope."[25]

---

23. Manton, *Psalm 119*, 6:138; 8:12–13. For more on Puritan meditation, see J. Stephen Yuille, "Conversing with God's Word: Scripture Meditation in the Piety of George Swinnock," *Journal of Spiritual Formation and Soul Care* 5 (2012): 35–55.

24. Manton, *Psalm 119*, 7:391–92, 96. Manton adds, "The whole drift of our religion is to call us off from time to eternity, from this world to a better" (*Psalm 119*, 7:398).

25. Manton, *Psalm 119*, 7:399.

For this reason, we must set "eternal things" before us—on the one side there are "eternal joys" and "solid godliness," while on the other side there are "eternal torments" and "vain pleasures." Having considered these things, we take the eternal God as our portion, seeking to "do all things from eternal principles to eternal ends." This, for Manton, is how biblical meditation works. In sum, it "is not a flourishing of the wit, that we may please the fancy by playing with divine truths ... but a serious inculcation of them upon the heart, that we may urge it to practice."[26]

THE PRACTICE OF MEDITATION

In Manton's approach to meditation it is crucial that the three principal faculties of the soul (mind, affections, and will) are engaged.[27] He maintains that the soul consists of faculties that should "command and direct" (mind, affections, will) and faculties that should be "commanded and directed" (phantasy, appetite, sense).[28] By God's design, our mind is supposed to

---

26. Manton, *Psalm 119*, 6:138; 7:400. For some insight into Manton's emphasis on solitude, see Crawford Gribben, "Thomas Manton and the Spirituality of Solitude," *Eusebeia: The Bulletin of the Jonathan Edwards Centre for Reformed Spirituality* 6 (Spring 2007): 21–23.

27. A faculty-focused approach to meditation is widespread among the Puritans. J. I. Packer observes, "Knowing themselves to be creatures of thought, affection, and will, and knowing that God's way to the human heart (the will) is via the human head (the mind), the Puritans practiced meditation, discursive and systematic, on the whole range of biblical truth. ... In meditation the Puritan would seek to search and challenge his heart, stir his affections to hate sin and love righteousness, and encourage himself with God's promises." See Packer, *A Quest for Godliness: The Puritan Vision of the Christian Life* (Wheaton, IL: Crossway, 1990), 24. Horton Davies defines the goal of Puritan meditation as "moving from intellectual issues to exciting the heart's affections in order to free the will for conformity to God." See Davies, *Worship and Theology in England from Andrewes to Baxter and Fox, 1603–1690* (Princeton: Princeton University Press, 1975), 119. In a similar vein, Peter Toon states, "In meditation a channel is somehow opened between the mind, heart, and will—what the mind receives enters the heart and goes into action via the will." See Toon, *From Mind to Heart: Christian Meditation Today* (Grand Rapids: Baker Books, 1987), 18. In terms of the affections specifically, he states, "Meditation was seen as a divinely appointed way of stimulating or raising the affections toward the glory of God" (*From Mind to Heart*, 94).

28. Manton, *Psalm 119*, 9:304. Manton holds to a bipartite view of humanity—it is body and soul. See, for example, *Sermon on Ecclesiastes 12:7, CWTM* 19:61–64. Some texts of Scripture seem to indicate that we are tripartite in nature: body, soul, and spirit (Matt 22:37; 1 Thess 5:23; Heb 4:12). According to this view, the soul is the seat of self-consciousness, whereas the spirit is the seat of God-consciousness. Manton disagrees. He believes the terms "soul" and "spirit" are used to note "the theological distinction of the faculties" (*Exposition of Jude, CWTM* 5:28). It is worth noting that, in Scripture, the expressions "body and soul" and "body and

counsel and command our affections. These, in turn, are supposed to move our phantasy (or imagination), which then controls our senses and the members of our body. As a result of the fall, however, this order has been corrupted. The commanding faculties are now "blind and sleepy," while the commanded faculties are now "obstinate" and "rebellious." This means that "bodily pleasure" now affects the senses; the senses move the phantasy; the phantasy controls the affections; and the affections blind the mind and captivate the will. As a result of this corruption, we are "carried headlong" to destruction.[29]

By God's grace, regeneration restores some order to the relationship among the commanding and commanded faculties; however, it does not perfect them. As a result, even in a regenerate state, we still struggle with disordered faculties. For this reason, we must engage in faculty-focused meditation. Beginning with the mind, we seek to discern the meaning of God's word.[30] We do not engage in a subjective reading of Scripture, seeking some sort of intuitive response, nor do we engage in a rationalistic reading

spirit" are used to refer to the whole person (Matt 10:28; 1 Cor 7:34; 2 Cor. 7:1; Jas 2:26). Plus, the terms "soul" and "spirit" are used interchangeably. Grief and sorrow are experienced in both (1 Kgs 21:5; Ps 42:11; Matt 26:38; Mark 8:12; John 12:27; 13:21; Acts 17:16; 2 Pet 2:8). Joy and spiritual desire are experienced in both (Pss 42:1–5; 63:3; 103:1–2; 116:7; 130:6; Isa 26:9; Luke 1:46–47). Devotion to God is experienced in both (Mark 12:30; Acts 4:32; 14:22; Eph 6:6; Phil 1:27).

29. Manton, *Psalm 119*, 9:304–6. Manton adds, "Our affections are so apt to be led by sense and not by right reason, that there is many times great danger that in seeing we should not see, lest seeing, knowing, and approving that which is better, we should embrace and follow that which is worse act contrary to our knowledge and conscience" (*Psalm 119*, 9:308–9).

30. For Manton, meditation necessarily involves the mind. This sets it apart from contemplation—the "supernatural elevation of the mind, by which it adhereth to God, and pauseth in the sight of God and glory without any variety of discourse; the soul being dazzled with the majesty of God, or the glory of heaven, and transported into a present joy." During these times, "the use of reason is for a time suspended, and the soul is cast into a kind of sleep and quietness of intuition, staring and gazing with ravishing sweetness upon the divine excellences and glory of our hope" (*Sermons on Genesis 24:63*, 293). Manton does not believe we should expect such experiences today. However, God does occasionally grant a measure of the beatific vision in the present, which results in "strong pangs and ecstasies of love, which for a while do suspend and forbid the distinct use of reason, and cast the soul into a quiet silent gaze." In this condition, "the soul falleth into the arms of Christ, and claspeth about Christ with the arms of its own love" (*Sermons on Genesis 24:63*, 294–95). For an analysis of the Puritan focus on the beatific vision, see Joel R. Beeke and Mark Jones, *A Puritan Theology* (Grand Rapids: Reformation Heritage Books, 2012), 824–25.

of Scripture, losing sight of the fact that it is God's word for God's people. Rather, we commit ourselves to the hard work of study while applying our minds to reflect on the wonder of God's truth as it emerges from his word. This results in "pregnant thoughts."[31]

From here, meditation moves to the affections. According to Manton, "our affections follow our apprehensions" because there is no way to come to the heart but by the mind.[32] If we remove the pot of water from the fire before it boils, it quickly cools. Similarly, if we end meditation before the affections are fully engaged, our enthusiasm quickly wanes. The way to engage the affections is by means of "serious enforcements" such as "arguments" (considering cause and effect), "similitudes" (using "sensible things" to understand "spiritual things"), "comparisons" (placing "contraries" together for the purpose of illustration), and "colloquies and soliloquies" (asking questions of ourselves).[33] These "serious enforcements" then work on the "two great influencing affections—love and hatred." The first serves for "choice and pursuit," while the second serves for "flight and aversion." The principal work of meditation is to fix these two on "their proper objects." Manton exhorts, "Our faith, our love, our desires, our delight, they are all acted and exercised by our thoughts; so that the spiritual life is but an imagination, unless we do frequently and often take time for serious meditation."[34]

Once "the two great influencing affections" are fixed on their proper objects, the will follows accordingly. It chooses what these affections (love and hatred) deem to be good and evil. When love is set on God and hatred is set on sin, the motions of the soul function properly. As a result, we take God as our happiness, his Son as our Savior, his Spirit as our guide, his word as our rule, his holiness as our desire, and his promises as our hope. In this way, then, the door is opened between the mind, affections, and will.

---

31. Manton, *Sermons on Genesis 24:63*, 303.
32. Manton, *Psalm 119*, 8:61–62.
33. Manton, *Sermons on Genesis 24:63*, 304.
34. Manton, *Psalm 119*, 7:80; 8:155.

THE FOCUS OF MEDITATION

Two important emphases emerge from Manton's faculty-focused approach to meditation. The first is his insistence that the mind be fixed on the right object. As the psalmist prays, "I will meditate on your wondrous works" (Ps 119:27). For Manton, God's word displays his "wondrous works," thereby furnishing us with numerous motifs worthy of our meditation. Specifically, we meditate on (1) "God, that we may love him and fear him"; (2) "sin, that we may abhor it"; (3) "hell, that we may avoid it"; and (4) "heaven, that we may pursue it." Manton adds, "Meditate upon the doctrines, promises, threatenings, man's misery, deliverance by Christ, necessity of regeneration, then of a holy life, the day of judgment. Fill the mind with such kind of thoughts, and continually dwell on them."[35]

One of the most profitable subjects for meditation is God himself. "I have remembered your name in the night, O Lord, and keep your law" (Ps 119:55).[36] In his sermon on this verse, Manton notes the psalmist's practice: "I have remembered your name in the night, O lord." Because the psalmist is "addicted to God," his heart is always "working towards God day and night," meaning he remembers God's name. Manton affirms that there is a twofold remembrance. The first is "notional and speculative" when we recall things with the mind; it consists of "barren notions" and "sapless opinions." The second is "practical and affective" when we recall things with the heart; it consists of "lively and powerful impressions" that produce "reverence, love, and obedience." In short, "we remember God so as to love him, and fear him, and trust in him, and make him our delight, and cleave to him, and obey him."[37]

---

35. Manton, *Psalm 119*, 6:144; 7:481. Elsewhere, Manton mentions the following subjects as worthy of meditation: the great end of man, the evil of sin, the misery of the world, the vanity of the creature, the horror of death, the severity of judgment, the torment of hell, the excellencies of Christ, the privileges of the gospel, the mystery of providence, and the glory of heaven (*Sermons on Genesis 24:63*, 303).

36. For the psalmist's remembrance of God's word, see Ps 119:22, 30, 44, 51, 55–56, 59–61, 67, 69, 83, 87–88, 93–94, 100–102, 104, 109–10, 115, 117, 129, 141, 153, 157, 161, 166, 168, 173, 176. Christ also figures prominently in Manton's meditation. By way of example, see *Exposition of Isaiah 53*, *CWTM* 3:187–494.

37. Manton, *Psalm 119*, 7:76–78.

This is done by keeping our thoughts on God until "we admire him [and] make some practical improvement of him." Manton enumerates various "improvements." First, an admiration of God draws us away from the creature by causing us to abase "all things beside God, not only in opinion but affection." Second, it draws us away from self by revealing our "vileness and misery" in the light of God's glorious majesty. Third, it draws us away from sin by showing us that it is "a deformity to God." Fourth, it draws us to him in faith, love, and fear.[38] For Manton, these three "radical" graces are the principal result of keeping the mind fixed on God—in short, thoughts of God's *power* produce *fear*, thoughts of his *wisdom* produce *faith*, and thoughts of his *goodness* produce *love*.[39]

THE FRUIT OF MEDITATION

The second essential component of Manton's faculty-focused approach to meditation is related to its fruit. "Those that do often and seriously keep God in their thoughts," writes Manton, "will be most careful to keep his commandments."[40] His reasoning is as follows: meditation enflames the three "radical" graces (i.e., faith, love, and fear), which, in turn, fuel obedience.

---

38. Manton, *Psalm 119*, 7:92–93.

39. Manton, *Sermons on 2 Corinthians 5*, *CWTM* 13:148. Manton comments, "This is the blessed employment of the saints, that they may live in the consideration and admiration of this wonderful love" (*Psalm 119*, 7:89). For Manton, this "rapturous" experience is depicted in the Song of Solomon (*Sermons on Genesis 24:63*, 301–4). He inherits this view from Bernard of Clairvaux. For a concise study of Bernard's spirituality of mystical union, as derived from the Song of Songs, see Arie de Reuver, *Sweet Communion: Trajectories of Spirituality from the Middle Ages through the Further Reformation*, trans. James A. De Jong (Grand Rapids: Baker Academic, 2007), 27–63. Manton is careful to acknowledge that these raptures are not "duties" to be pursued, but "experiences" to be enjoyed. For our part, we are to "content ourselves with grace, and peace, and joy in the Holy Ghost" (*Sermons on Genesis 24:63*, 297).

40. Manton, *Psalm 119*, 7:80. See Josh 1:8; Phil 4:8–9. The relationship between meditation and obedience, and the consequent blessing, is developed in Ps 1. The "blessed" man meditates on God's law "day and night" (v. 2). The verb "meditate" is a frequentative imperfect; hence, it is a continuous act. Thus, the righteous man is characterized by a daily routine of meditation on God's word. Interestingly, the conjunction "and" in verse 3 is part of a strong *waw* consecutive verb. This indicates the presence of a result clause. In other words, the individual who meditates on God's word is blessed. How? There is a fourfold description in verse 3. He is blessed because (1) he is like a tree planted by rivers of water, (2) he brings forth fruit in season, (3) his leaf does not wither, and (4) he prospers in whatever he does.

When the soul's faculties are rightly governed, practice follows affection, which follows persuasion, which follows knowledge. Because of the fall, however, this order has been "subverted." By this, Manton means that "objects strike upon the senses, sense moveth the fancy, fancy moveth the bodily spirits, the bodily spirits move the affections, and these blind the mind and lead the will captive." In this condition, our senses have become the "*cinque ports*" by which sin is let out and taken in."[41] When they hold sway, we lose sight of God's goodness, greatness, righteousness, and lovingkindness, the majesty of Christ, the beauty of grace, and the reality of eternity. These truths become mere *abstractions* and, as a result, our affections lose order, our mind loses focus, and our will chooses sin.

The only remedy for this predicament is meditation: "the mother and nurse of knowledge and godliness."[42] It helps the work of grace upon the understanding: "Continual meditation maketh religious thoughts actual and present." It helps the work of grace on the affections: "Serious meditation hath this advantage, that it doth make the object present, and as it were sensible." These "ponderous thoughts" become "bellows that kindle and inflame the affections." And it helps the work of grace on the life: "It maketh the heavenly life more easy, more sweet, more orderly and prudent."[43]

Manton sees this relationship between *knowledge* and *godliness* exemplified in Psalm 119:11, where the psalmist declares, "I have stored up your word in my heart, that I might not sin against you." In his sermon on this verse, Manton notes, first, the psalmist's *practice*: "I have stored up your word in my heart." We store up things in one of two ways—either to conceal them or cherish them. Manton believes the latter is in view: "What we value most preciously we save most carefully." We store God's word in our hearts through "knowledge" of it, "assent" to it, and "serious and sound digestion of it." That is to say, we do not study God's word in a "cursory manner," for a mere acquaintance with God's word will not do us any good; instead, we "ponder it seriously, that it may enter into [our] very heart." Manton notes,

41. Manton, *Psalm 119*, 6:351, 389–90.

42. Manton, *Psalm 119*, 9:80.

43. Manton, *Sermons on Genesis 24:63*, 274–77.

second, the psalmist's *purpose*: "that I might not sin against you." How does "storing up the Word" inhibit sin? For starters, it prevents "vain thoughts" because "the mind works upon what it finds in itself." It also urges us to duty, "restraining" us from sin and "directing" us in God's ways. Finally, it guards us "against temptations" by furnishing us the strength required to mortify the flesh.[44]

THE RULES FOR MEDITATION

It is evident from the above discussion that, for Manton, true knowledge is not restricted to the mind but manifests itself in life. In his own words, it "does not only stay in the fancy [or] float in the brain" but it "affects the heart." True knowledge is "operative," meaning it produces "a change both in the inward and outward man," whereby our practice is brought into greater conformity with God's word.[45] This is the great end of meditation—namely, to impress God's truth on our hearts, thereby resulting in obedience. This conviction is clearly evident in Manton's twelve "rules for meditation":

1. Whatever you meditate upon must be drawn down to application (Job 5:27).

2. Do not pry further than God hath revealed; your thoughts must be still bounded by the word.

3. When you meditate of God you must do it with great care and reverence; his perfections are matter rather of admiration than inquiry.

4. In meditating on common things, keep in mind a spiritual purpose.

---

44. Manton, *Psalm 119*, 6:99–102, 106.
45. Manton, *Psalm 119*, 6:118; 7:271.

5. Take heed of creating a snare to your souls. Some sins are catching, like fire in straw, and we cannot think of them without infection and temptation.

6. Meditate of those things especially which you have most need of. ... Seasonable thoughts have the greatest influence.

7. Whatever you meditate upon, take heed of slightness. ... A glance doth not discover the worth of anything.

8. Come not off from holy thoughts till you find profit by them, either sweet tastes and relishes of the love of God, or high affections kindled towards God, or strong resolutions begotten in yourselves.

9. Be thankful to God when he blesseth you in meditation, or else you will find difficulty in the next.

10. Do not bridle up the free spirit by rules of method. That which God calleth for is religion, not logic. ... Voluntary and free meditations are most smart and pregnant.

11. Your success in the duty is not to be measured by the multitude and subtlety of the thoughts, but the sincerity of them.

12. You must begin and end all with prayer. Duties are subservient one to another. In the beginning you must pray for a blessing upon the duty, and in the end commend your souls and resolutions to God.[46]

---

46. Manton, *Sermons on Genesis 24:63*, 277–81.

In these rules, Manton does not insist on a particular method of meditation, but a purposeful approach to meditation. His intention is to encourage the cultivation of practical knowledge—that which engages the commanding faculties of the soul.

CONCLUSION

The purpose of this chapter has been to consider Thomas Manton's understanding of meditation. It figures so prominently in his piety because he is convinced that it fastens God's word on the "mind and memory," reveals the "beauty" of divine truth, prevents "vain thoughts," and nurtures all "knowledge and godliness." It is, therefore, "not a thing of arbitrary concernment … but of absolute use, without which all graces wither."[47]

Manton's conviction is related directly to his concept of the spiritual life as the impression of God's goodness on us and our corresponding experience of "well-pleasedness," which feeds faith—the fountain of all graces (e.g., love, hope, and patience) and effects (e.g., spiritual sense, strength, and affection). For Manton, this impression of God's goodness comes by only one means: God's word.[48] The implication is obvious: meditation on God's word stands at the center of the spiritual life as "the great fuel of faith."[49]

---

47. Manton, *Psalm 119*, 6:141, 43. Also see *Psalm 119*, 7:19, 479–82; 8:12–13.
48. Manton, *Sermons on 2 Thessalonians 1:3*, 126.
49. Manton, *Sermons on Hebrews 11*, 376–77.

"A PATIENT WEARING OF CHRIST'S CROSS"

Hercules Collins and a
Baptist Theology of Persecution

STEVE WEAVER

In his chapter on the period in *The English Baptists of the Seventeenth Century*, B. R. White, the doyen of seventeenth-century English Baptist studies, has labeled 1660–88 as "The Era of the Great Persecution."[1] During this period all dissenters, including the Baptists, were persecuted.[2] As a result a rich body of literature was produced that reflects a vibrant spirituality. This chapter will seek to demonstrate that the prison writings of one seventeenth-century English Particular Baptist provide a window for a better understanding of both spirituality and a theology of persecution for that larger body of Baptists. These writings are characterized by confidence in the sovereign providence of God, a thankfulness for both physical and spiritual blessings, reflection on the sufficiency of Christ, and a certain expectation of a future deliverance and reward. It will further argue that only such a vibrant

---

1. B. R. White, *The English Baptists of the Seventeenth Century* (Didcot, UK: Baptist Historical Society, 1996), 95–133.

2. For an excellent study of this era, see Gerald R. Cragg, *Puritanism in the Period of the Great Persecution 1660–1688* (Cambridge: Cambridge University Press, 1957). See also Michael R. Watts, *The Dissenters*, vol. 1, *From the Reformation to the French Revolution* (Oxford: Clarendon, 1978), 221–62.

spirituality will suffice to sustain one in times of persecution. Before looking at these writings, however, it is important to consider the significance of their author and something of the historical context in which they were produced.

THE SIGNIFICANCE OF HERCULES COLLINS

The significance of Hercules Collins (1647–1702) among the Particular Baptists of the late seventeenth century can be seen in at least three areas.[3] First, he was a relatively prolific author among the Particular Baptists of the period, publishing at least twelve distinct works between 1680 and 1702.[4] Second, Collins was among the original signatories of the Second London Confession of Faith (1689). Third, Collins's name was affixed to the recommendatory epistle of *The Gospel Minister's Maintenance Vindicated* along with ten other prominent London Baptist pastors, including such luminaries as Benjamin Keach, Hanserd Knollys, and William Kiffin.[5] Combined, these facts demonstrate not only that Collins was an important figure in late seventeenth-century Baptist life, but that he can also serve as a faithful representative of the broader Baptist community.

HISTORICAL SETTING

Although Charles II had promised religious toleration when he returned to the throne following the Commonwealth protectorate of Oliver Cromwell, hopes for such were short-lived among the dissenters. It is unknown whether Charles II had any intention of keeping his promise of religious liberty. What

---

3. For details on the life and theology of Hercules Collins, see G. Stephen Weaver Jr., *Orthodox, Puritan, Baptist: Hercules Collins (1647–1702) and Particular Baptist Identity in Early Modern England* (Göttingen: Vandenhoeck & Ruprecht, 2015). For shorter treatments of the life of Collins, see Michael A. G. Haykin, "The Piety of Hercules Collins (1646/7–1702)," in *Devoted to the Service of the Temple: Piety, Persecution, and Ministry in the Writings of Hercules Collins*, ed. Michael A. G. Haykin and Steve Weaver (Grand Rapids: Reformation Heritage Books, 2007), 1–30; Haykin, "Collins, Hercules (d. 1702)," in the *Oxford Dictionary of National Biography*, ed. H. C. G. Matthew and Brian Harrison (Oxford: Oxford University Press, 2004), s.v.; and Haykin, "Hercules Collins and the Art of Preaching," in *A Cloud of Witnesses: Calvinistic Baptists in the 18th Century* (Darlington, UK: Evangelical Times, 2006), 21–26.

4. The only author during this period who could rival his production being his friend Benjamin Keach (1640–1704), pastor of the Horsley-Down congregation. For more on Keach, see Austin Walker, *The Excellent Benjamin Keach* (Dundas, ON: Joshua, 2004).

5. Benjamin Keach, *The Gospel Minister's Maintenance Vindicated* (London, 1689).

is known, however, is that Parliament passed a series of laws between 1661 and 1665 known as the Clarendon Code, which were designed to enforce conformity to the worship of the Church of England. The Corporation Act of 1661 required that person had to have received the sacrament of the Lord's Supper in the Church of England within the past year to be eligible for election to any government office. Eligible persons were also required to take the Oaths of Allegiance and Supremacy to the king of England. The Act of Uniformity of 1662 resulted in the ejection of approximately two thousand Puritan ministers from their pulpits, since it required complete subscription to the *Book of Common Prayer*. Most Puritan ministers resigned rather than conform to these demands. The Conventicle Act of 1664 forbade the assembling of five or more persons for religious worship other than Anglican. This in essence outlawed dissenting churches. The Five Mile Act of 1665 forbade any nonconforming preacher or teacher to come within five miles of a city or corporate town where he had previously served as a minister. All of these acts were aimed at stamping out both the dissenters and Catholics. Baptists were particularly hit hard by these laws, since they made their conscientious worship of God illegal.[6] One of the Baptists whose life and ministry was affected by these laws was Hercules Collins.

Collins served from 1677 until his death in 1702 as the pastor of London's oldest Baptist church,[7] which was then meeting in the Wapping area of London. For the first half of Collins's ministry (until the Act of Toleration in 1689) the congregation had to meet in secret for fear of persecution. Spies and informers were employed by the government and given large sums of money for the discovery of dissenting congregations.[8] English Baptist historian Joseph Ivimey records that the meetinghouse of Collins's congregation was attacked during this period, with the pulpit and pews being destroyed and windows smashed.[9] On July 9, 1683, Collins was indicted

---

6. For a fuller description of these acts and their impact on Baptists, see Ernest A. Payne and Norman S. Moon, *Baptists and 1662* (London, Carey Kingsgate, 1962).

7. See Ernest F. Kevan, *London's Oldest Baptist Church* (London, Kingsgate, 1933), for the remarkable first three hundred years of history of this congregation.

8. Kevan, *London's Oldest Baptist Church*, 43.

9. Joseph Ivimey, *A History of the English Baptists* (London, 1814), 2:448–49.

for failure to attend his local parish church.[10] But it was for his violation
of the Five Mile Act that Collins was actually imprisoned in 1684 at the
Newgate Prison.[11] Collins had addressed the Church of England in 1682
in a hypothetical conversation between a conformist and a nonconformist
by declaring, "If you do persecute us for our Conscience, I hope God will
give us that Grace which may inable us patiently to suffer for Christ's sake."[12]
Apparently God granted this desire, since English Baptist historian Thomas
Crosby, writing within forty years of Collins's death, records that he was
"a faithful minister of the gospel; though he had not a learned education,
yet was a useful and laborious servant of Christ, and one that suffered
imprisonment for his sake. He began to be religious early, and continued
faithful to the last, and was not shocked by the fury of persecutors."[13] It
was while he was in the infamous Newgate Prison that Collins penned two
of the most devotional of his twelve writings.[14] These two works will be the
focus of the remainder of this chapter.

THE PRISON WRITINGS

Though there are no indications of which was published first, the first work
considered here is *Counsel for the Living, Occasioned from the Dead*. This work was
a discourse on Job 3:17–18 that was written on the occasion of the deaths
of two of Collins's fellow prisoners at Newgate: Francis Bampfield and
Zachariah Ralphson.[15] Both apparently died in early 1684, when Collins

10. Middlesex County Record Society, *Rolls, Books, and Certificates ... 1667–1688*, vol. 4, ed. J. C. Jeaffreson (London, Chapman & Hall, 1892).

11. For a description of the horrors of the Newgate Prison during the seventeenth century, see Haykin, "Piety of Hercules Collins," 14.

12. Hercules Collins, *Some Reasons for Separation from the Communion of the Church of England, and the Unreasonableness of Persecution Upon that Account. Soberly Debated in a Dialogue between a Conformist, and a Nonconformist (Baptist.)* (London: John How, 1682), 20. In all quotations in this chapter from seventeenth-century sources, original spelling, punctuation, and capitalization have been retained.

13. Thomas Crosby, *The History of the English Baptists* (London: John Robinson, 1740), 129.

14. A complete list of Collins's works can be found in Haykin and Weaver, *Devoted to the Service of the Temple*, 135–37.

15. For biographical details on Bampfield, see Richard L. Greaves, "'Making the Laws of Christ His Only Rule': Francis Bampfield, Sabbatarian Reformer," in *Saints and Rebels: Seven Nonconformists in Stuart England* (Macon, GA: Mercer University Press, 1985), 179–210. Ralphson

was also imprisoned.[16] The text states, regarding the eternal state, "There the wicked cease from troubling; and there the weary be at rest. There the prisoners rest together; they hear not the voice of the oppressor" (AV). Collins summarizes these verses as consisting of three components: "first the Subjects; which are *Oppressors and Oppressed*: Secondly, The Predicate, *They shall Rest*: Thirdly, the *Receptacle*, or place of Rest, that's the *Grave*."[17]

Collins's work focuses on two aspects of "counsel" from Job 3:17–18, namely, the future judgment of the persecutors and the corresponding relief of the persecuted. Collins believed that both ideas present in these verses were pertinent for his times. The persecuted needed to be encouraged by the fact that one day the persecutors would be stopped and they would experience relief, if not in this life then in the life to come. Persecutors needed to realize that they would one day be judged for their mistreatment of the people of God. Collins's primary purpose in this discourse, however, was to provide comfort to persecuted Christians. This is seen in that at the end of the book he exhorts his readers to follow the apostle Paul's advice at the end of his discourse on the resurrection of saints in 1 Thessalonians 4 to "comfort one another with these words." Collins concludes his *Counsel for the Living* by exhorting his readers with these words: "While Sin, Satan, and an Unkind World is Discomforting you, do you in a lively Hope of the Resurrection of the Body, the coming of Christ, your Meeting of him, and continuing with him, cheer up and Comfort one another with these things."[18]

Before turning to offer comfort for the persecuted, Collins first indicts their persecutors as godless men. Collins characterizes the persecutors of Christians as wicked men who "are troublers of the *Church*." As such they are

---

was the alias of Jeremiah Mardsen. For biographical details on Ralphson, see R. L. Greaves, "Marsden, *(alias* Ralphson), Jeremiah (1624–1684)," in *Biographical Dictionary of British Radicals*, ed. Richard L. Greaves and Robert Zaller (Brighton, UK: Harvester, 1984), 2:214–15.

16. Keith Durso dates the death of Bampfield to February 16, 1684. See Durso, *No Armor for the Back: Baptist Prison Writings, 1600s–1700s* (Macon, GA: Mercer University Press, 2007), 105. For a transcript of the proceedings of the trials of Ralphson and Bampfield, see *Old Bailey Proceedings Online*, www.oldbaileyonline.org (accessed May 20, 2010), January 1684, trials of Zachariah Ralphson (t16840116–18) and Francis Bampfield (t16840116–20).

17. *CL* 1–2.

18. *CL* 33–34.

"Strangers to Gospel Principles, to a Gospel Spirit, and Gospel Teachings."
Collins concludes that "a persecuting spirit is not of a Gospel-complexion."
Judgment is coming for these evildoers, who "shall be made to confess their
wickedness in not setting Gods People at liberty to Worship him; they shall
fall into mischief, and be silent in darkness, and turned into Hell, with
Nations which forget *God*." Note the "liberty to Worship him." Likewise,
Collins excoriates the persecutors elsewhere for arresting elderly men, "Men
of threescore, fourscore Years of Age, hurried to Prison for nothing else but
for worshipping their *God*."[19] This seems to have especially raised the ire of
Collins since Bampfield, one of the men whose death occasioned this sermon,
was almost seventy when arrested for what proved to be the final time.[20]

Saints, however, will be given rest. "The time is coming," Collins
asserts, when "God hath promised we shall no more hear the voice of the
Oppressor."[21] The saints "shall know no more Apprehendings ... nor hear
no more of, Take him Jaylor, keep him until he be cleared by due course of
Law; we shall have no more Bolts nor Bars then on us, no more looking for
the Keeper then, nor speaking to Friends through Iron-grates." The "rest"
referred to in Job 3:17–18 is a "Rest in Sleep, being then out of all sense of
care, trouble, pain, and all manner of distraction, so in like manner shall we
be in the Grave." This was the rest Bampfield and Ralphson had attained.

However, this is not the only relief from persecution that Collins
anticipates. His belief in the sovereign providence of God causes him to
declare: "We shall none of us stay a night beyond God's determination."
Therefore, prisoners can be content with their circumstances "though limited
to one Room, which was our Kitchin, our Cellar, our Lodging-Room, our
Parlour."[22] Like the apostle Paul, these persecuted believers had learned to
be content in "every State."[23] These prisoners believed "that place is best"
where their Father had willed them to be. Having their daily bread, they
confessed that "God is as good in Prison as out." Collins therefore exhorts his

---

19. *CL* 6–9, 15.
20. Haykin, "Piety of Hercules Collins," 15.
21. *CL* 21; see also 31.
22. *CL* 23, 25–26.
23. *CL* 26, citing Phil 4:11.

readers that God's promises are not just to be read, but their truths trusted and experienced. "Beloved, it is one thing to Read the Promises, another thing to trust upon God by them, and experience the truth of them."[24] These prisoners had experienced the promised presence and blessing of God in the prison cell, and Collins wanted to exhort other persecuted Christians to trust in the promises of their loving Father. Collins reminded his readers:

> Gods Providential Dealings with his people in this world, is like Chequer-work, there is the dark, as well as the light side of Providence, the most Refin'd and best State and Condition of the best Saints are mixed here; if we have some peace, we have some trouble; if we have large Comforts one day, we may expect a great degree of trouble another; least we should be exalted above measure, we must have a thorn in the flesh now and then.[25]

Trusting God's providence, Collins could confidently declare, "let men and Devils do their worst, God will in his own time loose the Prisoners."[26]

Not only were Collins and his fellow persecuted brothers content with their situation because of God's providence, but they were also deeply thankful for God's physical and spiritual blessings while jailed. Collins calls these blessings "Prison-comforts." They blessed God for his grace, which enabled them to have "as much peace and satisfaction" in their one room prison cell as when they had complete liberty to stroll through their houses, gardens, and the homes of friends. They were also thankful for God's daily physical provision for them. "Blessed be God we have bread for the day; as the day so our strength has been."[27]

These prisoners, however, were most grateful for their spiritual blessings. Chief among these blessings was the presence of Christ. Of his persecuted

---

24. *CL* 25–26.
25. *CL* 28.
26. *CL* 26.
27. *CL* 25.

brothers Collins could write: "How much of the Presence of Christ have they had to inable them to bear the Cross quietly, patiently, contentedly." These saints also rejoiced that though they were bound by physical shackles, they had been set free from the bondage of sin and death. "Again, let us bless God, though we are in the Prison of man, yet that we are delivered from the Spiritual prison of Sin and Satan, into the glorious liberty of the Children of God, and out of the Kingdom of darkness into the glorious light of the Gospel." They realized that "the darkness of a Material Prison is nothing to the darkness of a Spiritual one." In this spiritual freedom believers "may have Liberty in Bonds, light in Darkness, Peace in Trouble." It was the spiritual blessings that enabled the suffering servants of Christ to endure their trials. Collins explains how he and his fellow prisoners had personally experienced the soul-strengthening power of spiritual fellowship with the Father. "Communion with God by the Spirit is a good Cordial to keep up the heart from fainting in this valley of tears, until we come to our Mount of Joy, where there is no limits of Joy and Blessedness."[28]

A second work Hercules Collins published from his prison cell was *A Voice from the Prison*. This work is an extended meditation on Revelation 3:11, where Christ admonishes the church of Philadelphia with the words, "Behold, I come quickly: hold that fast which thou hast, that no man take thy crown" (AV). Collins addresses this sermon "To the Church of God, formerly Meeting in Old-Gravel-Lane Wapping, and all who were Strangers and Foreigners, but now Fellow Citizens with the Saints, and of the Household of God."

In this sermon, Collins draws from at least 213 passages of Scripture to encourage his congregation to stand firm in the face of persecution.[29] Collins urges his besieged flock to not abandon the cause of Christ. "*Hold fast what thou hast*, when Satan would pull thy souls good from thee; when Relations, Husband, Wife, Children call upon you, and perswade you because of danger to cease from the work of the Lord, then hold fast."[30] Collins offers as

28. *CL* 25–28.
29. Durso, *No Armor for the Back*, 169.
30. *VP* 4.

a motivation for holding fast to Christ and his work that the one who stands fast will hear Christ profess to the Father on the day of judgment the words:

These are they which have continued with me in my Temptation; therefore I appoint unto you a Kingdom; therefore, because you owned me in an Evil Day. These are the Men, Woman, People, which spoke of my Testimonies before Kings, and was not ashamed when many Cried, Crucify him and his Cause; these are the souls which came forth and declared they were on the Lords Side: These are they, Father, whose Love to me many Waters nor Floods could not quench nor drown; these have made Choice of me with Reproaches, Imprisonments, with Fines, Confiscation of Goods, Banishment, loss of Limbs, Life, and all, they have born all, endured all for my sake, in the greatest affliction, they kept from wavering, and the more they endured and lost for my sake, the more they loved me.[31]

Just as Collins had encouraged persecuted believers in his *Counsel for the Living* to not give in because of the future rest which awaited them, so too in *A Voice from the Prison* he exhorts them to live in view of their future appearance before God's judgment seat.

Collins also drew comfort from God's sovereign providence during his imprisonment. He begins his written address to his "Dearly Beloved" church by expressing his confidence that God is providentially at work in his suffering for the advancement of the gospel.

Forasmuch as I am present depriv'd by my Bonds, of the Liberty of Preaching; I bless God I have the Advantage of Printing, being ready to serve the Interest of Christ in all Conditions to my poor Ability; and doubt not, but God and Interest are Served by my Confinement, as by Liberty:

---

31. *VP* 5.

and am not without hopes that I shall preach as loudly, and
as effectually by Imprisonment for Christ, as ever I did
at Liberty; that all those who observe Gods Providential
Dealings, will be able to say with me hereafter, as Holy *Paul*
once said in his Bonds at *Rome*; What hath befallen me, hath
tended to the furtherance of the Gospel.[32]

Like the apostle Paul in Philippians 1, Collins's belief in the providence of
God caused him to have confidence that God would bring good out of his
imprisonment. One of the goods that Collins believed could come out of
the sufferings of the Baptists was that some of their adversaries might be
convinced by how they patiently endured when persecuted. He argued that
since "Actions are more Influential then words, and more Demonstrative of
the Truth and Reality of a Person or Cause" and "as a man shall be better
believed for his good works, then good words," suffering patiently would
convince their persecutors. Collins therefore encourages his congregation,
"So if we would Manifest our Integrity under a Profession, nothing will do
it better then your Suffering … if by God called unto it; for, as a Tree is
known by his fruit, so is a Christian by a Patient Wearing Christs Cross, this
will and hath Convinced an Adversary, when a bare Profession will not."[33]

In a similar manner, in *Counsel for the Living*, Collins maintains that God
can "make people grow so much the more as their afflictions abound," for
"thinking people will conclude they must be the Lords, that suffer patiently
under such apparent wrong."[34] Therefore, Collins encourages his fellow
believers to "see how our Churches fill, come let us go on, we have good
success, we shall bring them all home at last."[35] This would apparently prove
to be true for Collins and his congregation, since by the time of his death
in 1702, as Michael A. G. Haykin has observed, Collins "was probably

---

32. *VP* 1.
33. *VP* 1.
34. *VP* 26.
35. *VP* 23.

preaching to a congregation of roughly 700 people, which would have made his congregation one of the largest Calvinistic Baptist works in the city."[36]

Collins also exhorts his readers to persevere, for God has promised to reward the overcomers. He then draws on all the promises made by Christ in Revelation 2–3 to those who persevere through persecution. The overcomers shall "eat of the Tree in the midst of the Paradice of God," "not be hurt of the Second Death," "have the hidden Manna," have "the white Stone, and a New name," "have power over the nations, and rule them with a Rod of Iron," and shall be "clothed in white Rayment." Their "name shall not be blotted out of the Book of Life, but made a Pillar in the Temple of God, and he shall go out no more." Finally, those who overcome "shall sit with Christ on his Throne, as he overcame and sat down with the Father on his Throne." These shall receive "a Crown not of Gold, but Glory, not fading but eternal."[37]

Collins knew that his readers would be able to "hold fast" if they were fully satisfied with Christ. "It is the Christ-finding Soul which is the Life-finding Soul." Collins explains that when it is said in Scripture, "Christ is all, and in all," that "he is all, because all good is Comprehended in him, he is all in all; all in the Fullness of all, for if we have all Earthly Injoyments, and have not him, we have nothing comparatively." However, to have Christ is to "have all Equivalently and comprehensively." Therefore, Collins warns that it is important to "hold fast this Christ." The world, he declares, will try to sink you if you held it too closely to your heart. "Cast away all, shake off all, rather then lose a Christ." True believers see God as "the Chief good, and Supream Happiness." Thus "will a Believing Soul suffer the Loss of all, so he may win Christ; none but Christ, saith an illuminated Believer."[38] Collins seems to speak on behalf of the "illuminated Believer" as he extols how this view of the sufficiency of Christ enabled him to endure hardships in this life.

---

36. Haykin, "Piety of Hercules Collins," 22.
37. *VP* 6.
38. *VP* 6, 8, 9, 18.

There are many good Objects in Heaven and Earth besides thee, there are Angels in Heaven, and Saints on Earth: But, what are these to thee? Heaven without thy Presence, would be no Heaven to me; a Pallace with thee, a Crown without thee, cannot satisfie me; but with thee I can be content, though in a poor Cottage with thee I am at Liberty in Bonds; Peace and Trouble; if I have thy Smiles, I can bear the worlds frowns; if I have Spiritual Liberty in my Soul, that I can ascend to thee by Faith, and have Communion with thee, thou shalt chuse my Portion for me in this World.[39]

Some, however, were apparently being tempted to abandon the all-sufficient Christ for a respite from the persecution. Collins warns that "without enduring to the End, all your Profession, your many years Prayers, all your Tears will be lost." Those who turn aside "mayst never more be called to be a witness for Christ," and "some have thought God hath not Lov'd them, because he hath not Exercised them this way." Elsewhere in this prison epistle, Collins soberly charges those who had been enabled by God's grace to persevere not to boast in their state. "To all such as have fallen in the Storm, who have kept their garments from Defiling, let God have the glory; thou standest by Faith, which God is Author of, be not High-minded but fear; glory not secretly, Rejoice not in thy Brothers fall." For those who have fallen, Collins offers a word of hope. "The Lord hath promised he will not let his Anger fall upon you … therefore, Return, Return … that we may look upon thee with Joy and Delight, as the Angels in Heaven do rejoice at the Returning of a Soul to God." Collins further exhorts his wayward readers to return into the arms of a merciful God. "Return to thy God from whom thou hast revolted, who stands with open Arms to receive you; return to the Church again, whom thou hast made sad by thy departing from the Truth, and humble thy self to God and them, and they will cheerfully receive thee into their fellowship."[40]

---

39. *VP* 18–19.
40. *VP* 3, 26, 28.

Saints will only be enabled to endure persecution who have first been putting to death the deeds of their flesh daily. "Let not that Man think to wear the Cross of Persecution, that doth not first wear the Cross of Mortification."[41] Collins expounds on this concept:

> We should inure our selves to wear the Publick Cross, by wearing it first more privately in our Houses, in our Families, in our Shops and Trades: For let not that Person think he will ever be able to part with his Houses, Lands, Liberties, for the Lord Jesus Christ, that cannot first part with a secret lust: But if we have Grace enough, to wear daily the Cross of Mortification of the old Man; you need not fear but he that giveth Grace to do the greater, will give Grace to doe the lesser; for I look upon the subduing of Corruption, a greater thing then enduring Persecution; though neither can be done as it ought, without help from Heaven.[42]

Those who, by the grace of God, were regularly putting to death their sins will experience an easier path in enduring physical persecution. Thus, Collins is encouraging personal holiness as the best means to prepare for persecution for the cause of Christ. Without this spiritual practice, professing believers will not be able to withstand the temptation to deny Christ in the face of persecution.

Collins closes his sermon from prison with a series of prayers. First, Collins prays that God will purge the church of its impurities, which he saw as a cause for their persecution. "God is contending with us: Let us all Banish and Expel the Achan out of our Hearts, out of our Churches, and shew our selves Zealous against Sin." Second, Collins prays that Christ's kingdom will come. "We should be willing to be Footstools, so Christ thereby might get upon his Throne." Third, Collins prays for "a universal spreading of the Gospel" in order that "a greater degree of Knowledge and Holiness

---

41. *VP* 30.
42. *VP* 30.

will be in the World then ever." Finally, Collins prays for deliverance. "We have no might, but our Eyes are upon thee. ... Appear in thy strength, that the Kingdoms of the World may know that thou art God; and that there is none besides thee." "In the mean time," Collins concludes his letter from prison, "let our Faith and Patience be lengthened out, to the coming of the Lord; till Time swallowed up in Eternity; Finite, in Infinite, Hope, in Vision; and Faith in Fruition; when God shall be the matter of our Happiness; when Fulness shall be the measure of our Happiness, and Eternity the Duration."[43]

CONCLUSION

The prison writings of Hercules Collins provide a window for better understanding both seventeenth-century English Baptist spirituality and a Baptist theology of persecution. The furnace of affliction revealed a deep and vibrant spirituality that was like pure gold. These golden writings are characterized by a confidence in the sovereign providence of God, a thankfulness for both physical and spiritual blessings, reflection on the sufficiency of Christ, and a certain expectation of a future deliverance and reward. It is hoped that a similar spirituality would become prominent among Baptists once again in order that they might be enabled to persevere through the persecution that increasingly seems certain to come.

---

43. *VP* 32.

THE SIXTH SENSE OF
JONATHAN EDWARDS

TOM J. NETTLES

Jonathan Edwards loved the theology of personal religious experience. Not only does he have four major works given largely to the task of describing—and also prescribing—the nature of religious experience as he observed it in others, but he indulges himself in teasing out the nature of his own experience. Edwards's "Diary" and his "Resolutions"[1] show a person determined to examine every motive, plan every thought, be responsible for every moment, the "improvement of precious time," take great care in every movement of the eye and expression of the face, and hold himself to give an account to himself for success or failure. On June 6, 1725, he wrote in his "Diary," "I am sometimes in a frame so listless, that there is no other way of profitably improving time, but conversation, visiting, or recreation, or some bodily exercise. However, it may be best in the first place, before resorting to either of these, to try the whole circle of my mental employments."[2] He felt the personal stewardship of destroying everything in his life that "raised itself against the knowledge of God" and to "take every thought captive to obey Christ" (2 Cor 10:5).

---

1. Jonathan Edwards, *Works of Jonathan Edwards* (repr., Edinburgh: Banner of Truth Trust, 1976), 1:xxiii–xxxvi; *JER* 266–74; *WJE* 16:753–59.

2. Edwards, *Works of Jonathan Edwards*, 1:xxxvi.

The analyses of the nature and progress of his own religious perceptions supplemented those he did of others, including particularly his critical observation of the spiritual life of his wife, Sarah Pierrepont Edwards, a remarkable person in her own right. In *Some Thoughts Concerning the Revival*, Edwards fills several pages with an extended observation of her spiritual experience for a period of about seven years. He calls her "the Person." He notes several things united in the person's experience, making pivotal the part that "sense" played in this unusual elevation of continual worship:

> A very frequent dwelling, for some considerable time together, in such views of the glory of the divine perfections, and Christ's excellencies, that the soul in the meantime has been as it were perfectly overwhelmed, and swallowed up with light and love and a sweet solace, rest and joy of soul, that was altogether unspeakable; and more than once continuing for five or six hours together, without any interruption, in that clear and lively view or sense of the infinite beauty and amiableness of Christ's person, and the heavenly sweetness of his excellent and transcendent love.[3]

References to sensory language as foundational to spiritual experience became commonplace in Edwards's provocative engagement with evidences of true Christianity. For this person he notes "views of the glory," "swallowed up with light," "sweet solace," "lively view or sense," and "heavenly sweetness." In his "Personal Narrative" one finds his introspection put in the vocabulary of "sensibility," a perceptive framework that appears frequently in his other writings and is sprinkled strategically throughout his sermons.

---

3. *WJE* 4:332. Volume 4 is "The Great Awakening," edited by C. C. Goen.

SENSIBILITY IN EDWARDS'S PERSONAL NARRATIVE

Defining Sensibility

In this personal narrative, Edwards points to May or June 1721 as the time when he could identify "that change by which I was brought to those new dispositions, and that new sense of things."[4]

He recalls that the first time he experienced "that sort of inward, sweet delight in God and divine things that I have lived much in since, was on reading those words 'Now unto the King eternal, immortal, invisible, the only wise God, be honour and glory for ever and ever, Amen.' " Those words brought into his soul a diffusion of "a sense of the glory of the Divine Being; a new sense, quite different from any thing I ever experienced before." The scriptural language conveyed to him a longing to enjoy that God and "be rapt up in him in heaven, and be as it were swallowed up in him for ever!" Though Edwards did not perceive that this "new sense" had anything saving in it at the time, he kept "singing over these words of scripture" and praying "that I might enjoy him" in an unprecedented manner and "with a new sort of affection."[5]

He observed that contemplating on the work of Christ and redemption prompted "an inward, sweet sense of these things," and his soul was "led away in pleasant views and contemplations on them." His readings and meditations, particularly those that included a christological application of the Song of Solomon, presented to him "the loveliness and beauty of Jesus Christ" with intense images of beauty and "an inward sweetness that would carry me away, in my contemplations." In short, "The sense I had of divine things, would often of a sudden kindle up, as it were, a sweet burning in my heart; an ardor of soul, that I know not how to express."[6]

These impressions stayed clearly with Edwards all his ministry, and through study were intensified and formed the basis of his life's work. His works on religious affections, the will, original sin, analysis of revival, true

---

4. *WJE* 16:790.

5. *WJE* 16:792, 793.

6. *WJE* 16:792–93.

virtue, and the purpose of creation all focused on the point of divine/human encounter: the excellence of the divine being and the "new sense of things" the human must grasp and the resultant relish for the holy beauty of God. Edwards did not see this as important only in terms of personal assurance, but also as an apologetic for the exclusive truth of Christianity. In the very first section of his "Observations on the facts and evidences of Christianity, and the objections of infidels" he says, "It is easily proved that the highest end and happiness of man is to view God's excellency, to love him, and receive expressions of his love. This love, including all those other affections which depend upon, and are necessarily connected with it, are expressed in worship."[7]

What does Edwards mean by a phrase such as "view God's excellency"? How does one realize one is a recipient of "expressions of his love"? When one speaks of a "new sense of things," how does this integrate with the objective historical events of Christianity and the doctrinal construction derived from a synthesis of objective divine revelation? One meets this concept of sensibility at every turn in Edwards. I will attempt a definition. "Sensibility" or a condition of being "sensible" is a state in which first the mind and then the affections are convinced of and approve a biblical idea as if the senses themselves had recorded it on the consciousness as an invincible and indelible fact.

Sometimes he uses the word for a state of sensibility into which a merely natural man may be brought by powerful working of the Spirit on the mind and conscience. Normally such a state of sensibility would be of the danger of condemnation in which an unforgiven sinner stands. Most often, the word refers to a state of true spiritual understanding arising from the Spirit's work of effectual calling or of some particular operations of his sanctifying influences. Edwards expresses this relation between natural and spiritual sensibility as he examines the ground of his assurance, fearing that he did "not feel the Christian graces sensibly enough." He goes on to explain that he fears they are "only such hypocritical outside affections which wicked men may feel as well as others." Then he continues his rumination by focusing

---

7. Edwards, *Works of Jonathan Edwards*, 2:460.

on the positive, spiritual substance of sensibility. He calls such perceptions "inward, full, sincere, entire, and hearty." They should be "substantial" and "wrought into my very nature."[8]

Ten Layers of Sensibility

In his "Personal Narrative" Edwards explains at least ten of these moments of sensibility. The first came when his early and strong objections to the doctrine of absolute divine sovereignty, a "horrible doctrine," were overcome in a sense of the rational perfection of such an idea. He could not explain how it happened. But now his "reason apprehended the justice and reasonableness of it," his mind "rested in it," and "all those cavils and objections came to an end."[9]

His second instance of the soul-altering power of "sensibility" came when he attained a "delightful conviction" of absolute sovereignty based on 1 Timothy 1:17. "Absolute sovereignty is what I love to ascribe to God." Later in Northampton, "The doctrines of God's absolute sovereignty, and free grace, in showing mercy to whom he would show mercy; and man's absolute dependence on the operations of God's Holy Spirit, have very often been much my delight." Absolute sovereignty was a "great part of his glory," and so, for Edwards, he found it "sweet to me to go to God, and adore him as a sovereign God, and ask sovereign mercy of him."[10]

A third advance prompted by increased sensibility involved "new apprehensions of Christ and the work of redemption, and the glorious way of salvation by him." In thinking about this, Edwards had "an inward sweet sense of these things, that at times came into my heart; and my soul was led away in pleasant views and contemplations of them." Deeper and more elongated periods of sensation about Christ punctuated Edwards's experience and prompted phrases such as "ineffably excellent" with an "excellency great enough to swallow up all thought and conception." He seemed to struggle with words sufficiently strong to express the "sense of the excellent fullness

8. *WJE* 16:759.
9. *WJE* 16:792; *JER* 283.
10. *WJE* 16:792, 799; *JER* 283, 291.

of Christ and his meetness and suitableness as a Saviour: whereby he has appeared to me, far above all, the chief of ten thousand." Christ's blood and atonement appeared "sweet, and his righteousness sweet" with such intensity and "ardency of spirit, and inward struggling and breathings and groaning, that cannot be uttered, to be emptied of myself, and swallowed up in Christ." Contemplation of Christ brought "an inward sweetness" and "a calm sweet abstraction of soul from all the concerns of this world."[11]

A fourth experience of sensibility involved a "sweet sense of the glorious majesty and grace of God." Edwards seemed "to see them both in sweet conjunction: majesty and meekness joined together." He writes of a "sweet and gentle, and holy majesty" and conversely viewed God in terms of "majestic meekness."[12] There is a peculiar beauty in meekness when it arises from infinite majesty and strength as well as a delightful and absorbing wonder in overwhelming majesty when it is displayed in gentle meekness.

Fifth, as Edwards's sense of the all-comprehending beauty of God increased, his "sense of divine things gradually increased, and became more and more lively." Edwards began to sense the divine beauty in everything— sun, moon, stars, sky, flowers, birds, insects, thunderstorms; "I felt God at the first appearance of a thunderstorm; and used to take the opportunity at such times, to fix myself to view the clouds, and see the lightnings play, and hear the majestic and awful voice of God's thunder; which oftentimes was exceeding entertaining." He would sing or chant his meditations and put his thoughts into soliloquies on viewing these natural phenomena.[13]

His move to New York prompted a sixth element of advance in his sense of the excellence of true Christianity. His "sense of divine things seemed gradually to increase" until he went to New York, when he felt "them very sensibly, in a much higher degree, than I had done before." This time the issue of holiness was paramount. His "longings after God and holiness were much increased." He panted after holiness here and perfection of holiness in heaven. His meditations led him to adore holiness, to seek lowliness as

---

11. *WJE* 16:793, 801; *JER* 292–93.
12. *WJE* 16:793; *JER* 285.
13. *WJE* 16:793–94; *JER* 285.

well as holiness, and to contemplate the holiness of heaven. "The heaven I desired," Edwards recounts, "was a heaven of holiness, to be with God, and to spend my eternity in divine love, and holy communion with Christ." He would sometimes say to himself, "I certainly know that I love holiness, such as the gospel prescribes." He saw nothing in holiness "but what was ravishingly lovely." On December 22, 1722, Edwards confided to his diary that he was "affected with a sense of the excellence of holiness." In conjunction with that, he also acknowledges that he "also felt sensible repentance of sin, because it was committed against so merciful and good a God."[14]

In a sermon titled "The Way of Holiness," Edwards opens his doctrine with the words, "Many are not sensible enough of the necessity of holiness in order to salvation." If all who wanted heaven went there, then it would be filled with murderers, adulterers, swearers, drunkards, and rogues of all sorts who see heaven not in terms of holiness but in terms of an endless continuation of their pursuit of sensual pleasure. To counteract this great misperception "it behooves us all to be sensible of the necessity of holiness in order to salvation." As Edwards spins out his explanation of this sensibility of holiness, he uses phrases such as "most inward, hearty, and sincere holiness"; sensibility of holiness is of such a nature that it "must become natural thus to be, and thus to act; it must be the constant inclination and new nature of the soul."[15] This conjunction of sensibility and the "new nature of the soul" shows that Edwards saw the Spirit's operation of conversion as identical with the penetration of one's spiritual apprehension, with sensibility of the pure glory, beauty, sweetness, and pleasantness of all the truth of divine revelation and the way of salvation by Christ.

In a seventh record Edwards gives of his sensible grasp of divinity, he points to the Bible and the doctrines of the gospel. "I felt harmony between something in my heart, and those sweet and powerful words [of the biblical text]. I seemed to see so much light, exhibited by every sentence, and such a ravishing food communicated, that I could not get along in reading." Then later, "The gospel has seemed to me the richest treasure; the treasure that I

14. *WJE* 16:759, 795–96; *JER* 287.
15. *SJE* 3–5.

have most desired, and longed that it might dwell richly in me. The way of salvation by Christ, has appeared in a general way, glorious and excellent, and most pleasant and beautiful." Still maintaining his contemplations of the power and beauty of Scripture and of the doctrine of the gospel, Edwards records, "I have sometimes had an affecting sense of the excellency of the Word of God, as a Word of life … accompanied with a thirsting after that word, that it might dwell richly in my heart."[16]

This kind of delight in the word of God points to Edwards's understanding of the relation between cognition and sense. These are two things. One is speculative and notional and involves analysis, intellectual engagement, and increasing in the grasp of the conceptual framework of ideas, and may be obtained by the "natural exercise of our own faculties, without any special illumination of the Spirit of God." This level of understanding is essential, and on it depends the other level of knowledge—sensibility. The more cognition one has, then the more elevated and intense may one's sensibility be. Spiritual understanding "rests not entirely in the head, or in the speculative ideas of things; but the heart is concerned in it: it principally consists in the sense of the heart." A right speculative knowledge of divinity is, therefore, to be pursued as a genuine mark of obedient discipleship, but the goal is to have a "due sense of them in the heart."[17]

While only one of these kinds of knowledge is saving, the other is of infinite importance, for "without it we can have no spiritual or practical knowledge." One cannot love an object that is entirely unknown, and "the heart cannot be set upon an object of which there is no idea in the understanding." Sensibility follows and depends on cognition. There is no spiritual knowledge where there is not first a rational knowledge. The spiritual senses cannot verify the truth and rightness of a thing without the thing being present to the mind. "He cannot have a taste of the sweetness and divine excellency of such and such things contained in divinity, unless he first have a notion that there are such and such things."[18]

---

16. *WJE* 16:797–801; *JER* 289–93.

17. *SJE* 30.

18. *SJE* 32.

An eighth identifiable distinction in Edwards's kaleidoscope of sensibilities is found in a sense of the glory and pleasantness of a "direct view of the glorious things of the gospel." Amazingly, Edwards called such a perspective "the sweetest joys and delights I have experienced." Far sweeter than any persuasion that he personally had, eternal benefit from the gospel was the direct contemplation of the symmetry, beauty, infinite glory, and divine worthiness of the gospel itself irrespective of his own safe estate in its provision. The purely objective, ontological beauty of God's scheme of redemption seemed to be pure "sweetness" that carried him "above the thoughts of my own safe estate."[19]

A ninth identifiable experience of sensibility pointed to the "glory of the third person in the Trinity," particularly his office as the sanctifier of unholy people in his "holy operations communicating divine light and life to the soul." The Spirit operates "sweetly and pleasantly" as an "infinite fountain of divine glory and sweetness being full and sufficient to fill and satisfy the soul."[20]

Deeply embedded in his entire experience was the tenth aspect of sensibility, which Edwards identifies as "too great a dependence on my own strength."[21] In moments of exhilaration about divine things, he could seem to transcend his intrinsic weakness and reality of indwelling sin but would then return to find that he was not yet in heaven. He identified this failure as "a great disadvantage to me." He came to recognize extreme feebleness and impotence in every way. This was not simply the juxtaposition of finite creatureliness to infinite, omnipotent divinity (a reality of which he was deeply sensible), but the weakening poison of indwelling sin, the "innumerable and bottomless depths of secret corruption and deceit." He had a powerful view of his own wickedness "like an abyss infinitely deeper than hell." "It is affecting to me to think," he reminded himself, "how ignorant I was, when I was a young Christian, of the bottomless, infinite depths of wickedness, pride, hypocrisy and deceit left in my heart." He expressed his

---

19. *WJE* 800; *JER* 292.
20. *WJE* 16:801; *JER* 293.
21. *JER* 287.

growing consciousness of being afflicted with "a proud and self-righteous spirit, much more sensibly, than I used to be formerly."[22]

In closing his *Personal Narrative*, Edwards gives a fitting summary of the diverse yet unified areas of sensibility in his Christian pilgrimage to that point.

Yet of late years, I have had a more full and constant sense of the absolute sovereignty of God, and a delight in that sovereignty; and have had more of a sense of the glory of Christ, as a mediator, as revealed in the gospel. On one Saturday night in particular, had a particular discovery of the excellency of the gospel of Christ, above all other doctrines; so that I could not but say to myself; "This is my chose light, my chosen doctrine": and of Christ, "This is my chosen prophet." It appeared to me to be sweet beyond all expression, to follow Christ, and to be taught and enlightened and instructed by him; to learn of him, and live to him.

Another Saturday night, January 1738/9, had such a sense, how sweet and blessed a thing it was, to walk in the way of duty, to do that which was right and meet to be done, and agreeable to the holy mind of God; that it caused me to break forth into a kind of a loud weeping, which held me some time; so that I was forced to shut myself up, and fasten the doors. I could not but as it were cry out, "How happy are they which do that which is right in the sight of God! They are blessed indeed, they are the happy ones!" I had at the same time, a very affecting sense, how meet and suitable it was that God should govern the world, and order all things according to his own pleasure; and I rejoiced in it, that God reigned, and that his will was done.[23]

---

22. *WJE* 16:802–33; *JER* 294–95.
23. *WJE* 16:803–4.

SENSIBILITY IN SERMONS

With this idea so inextricably entrenched in Edwards's personal experience
so that it informed all his ideas about true Christian experience, one would
expect to find the idea as elemental to his sermons. This is certainly the case
with "Sinners in the Hands of an Angry God." After stating his doctrine,
"There is nothing that keeps wicked men, at any one moment, out of hell,
but the mere pleasure of God," and then establishing its truthfulness by
ten rigorously reasoned doctrinal proofs that "God is under no manner of
obligation to keep him a moment from eternal destruction," he introduces
the applicatory phase of the sermon with the phrase, "You probably are
not sensible of this."[24] Edwards saw his task as a preacher to set forth the
cognitive foundation of truth with as much reasoning and exposition as he
could muster and to press the application with as many images, analogies,
metaphors, and similes as would make impressions on the senses:

> The wrath of God burns against them, their damnation
> don't slumber, the pit is prepared, the fire is made ready, the
> furnace is now hot, ready to receive them, the flames do
> now rage and glow. The glittering sword is whet, and held
> over them, and the pit hath opened her mouth under them.
> ... There are black clouds of God's wrath now hanging over
> your heads, full of the dreadful storm, and big with thunder.
> ... The corruption of the heart of man is a thing that is
> immoderate and boundless in its fury; and while wicked men
> live here, it is like fire pent up by God's restraints, when as if
> it were let loose it would set on fire the course of nature; and
> as the heart is now a sink of sin, so, if sin was not restrained,
> it would immediately turn the soul into a fiery over, or a
> furnace of fire and brimstone.[25]

24. *SJE* 55.
25. *SJE* 50–52.

Edwards had no delusion that such powerful images would be the immediate cause of conversion, for the granting of the new sense of things is purely an immediate operation of the divine Spirit. He did, however, see cognition as necessarily consistent with true spiritual understanding and thought that preaching should contain sensate images (feeling fire, smelling the stench of carrion, seeing glorious light distributed in beautiful colors and the flash of lightning, hearing a symphony of harmony or the lone voice of superlative melody or the shriek of persons in exquisite and incurable pain, tasting bitter herbs or the sweetness of honey) commensurate with the idea that the sensibility of spiritual truth is described in Scripture in terms of the senses through which spiritual knowledge comes ("He who has ears to hear, let him hear").

These same ideas and emphases appear in his sermon based on Genesis 19:14, "Warning of Future Punishment Don't Seem Real to the Wicked." The sermon focuses on why Lot's sons-in-law did not heed the warning of imminent destruction of Sodom. It was important to Edwards to tease out the concept of "realization," or how a stated proposition takes on the character of being real in a person's perceptions. His first point is to investigate "what it is to realize a thing." He makes the point quickly that "there are these two things in realizing a thing, or necessary in order to things seeming real to us: believing the truth of it, and having a sensible idea or apprehension of it." After looking at what it means to believe the truth of the proposition, he points to the second essential element, "that we have a lively and sensible idea or apprehension of it." Mundane daily experiences of sensibility show us the reality of the world and people around us, such as flowers, heat, dust, a person's face, the sound of a voice. In the sensory experience of all these things, "they seem real to us, as we have a plain and sensible idea of them." Concerning future things, however, true things that are not yet impressed on the senses, we apprehend only in a dull, faint, and distant way. For that reason, as well as for reasons concerning our intrinsic moral dullness, "the greater part of men have not a lively sensible apprehension of the wrath of God and of eternal punishment; it never was set before their eyes and brought into clear view."[26]

Edwards then spins out this concept of sensibility into several aspects of the reality of future punishment. First, "they han't a sensible apprehension of the nearness of future punishment" because "they han't a lively sense of the uncertainty of life." Second, "they han't a sensible apprehension of the manner of their punishment." They may hear of the pouring out of wrath while they stand in the company of wicked men and devils, but "knowing but little of the manner of the punishment, they ben't much disquieted by fears of it." Third, "they han't a lively sensible idea of the greatness of the punishment." They may hear such things as the dreadfulness of it, the horror of it, the enraged subject of it expressing in just holiness his consummate wrath arising from infinite power and unbound creativity, but "they never felt none of it … and so they have no notion how dreadful it is." Fourth, "they have no lively sensible apprehension of the eternity of this punishment." They have no idea of how they will be affected when, in the midst of unendurable torment, the thought also afflicts them that there be no end, no intermission, no diminishment, no hope of relief, no presence even of common mercies. "They have very little of an idea how such a despair will sink and oppress them and will feel like a mountain of lead that will fall upon them and crush them."[27]

This lack of sensibility explains why they do not heed warnings of future punishment. Like all other rational beings, should they realize the character of punishment, they would fear it greatly and seek ways to avoid it. This lively knowledge "would certainly terrify them and make them as uneasy as others, if they were equally sensible of their danger." In many temporal matters of calamitous implications for their well-being, "they can see with their eyes and they are very sensible how it would be with them, how miserable they should be if they should be poor, or if they should fall into disgrace

---

26. *WJE* 14:200–212. This volume is "Sermons and Discourses, 1723–1729," edited by Kenneth P. Minkema.

27. *WJE* 14:20–3.

and be laughed at." In such cases immediately present to their feelings and perceptions, "they are sensible it would be very ill with them in such a case."[28]

Doctrines of unseen things, especially of a spiritual nature and so immediately concerning their souls, are greatly diminished in their clarity by the stupefying effects of sin, so that these truths affect the minds of sinful men like seeds falling on a rock. That situation makes the idea of sensibility even more urgent. "They have been used to concern themselves only about sensible things, and used to depend upon their senses only; and therefore nothing seems real to them but what is sensible ... things that they can see and hear and feel and taste." For this reason, one of the tasks of the preacher is to take this into account and work toward the two components that make a thing "seem real to you: first to make you really believe that there is such a thing; and second, that you may have a more lively sensible apprehension of it."[29]

This idea constitutes a leading feature of the sermon "God Glorified in the Work of Redemption, by the Greatness of Man's dependence upon Him, in the Whole of It." The sinner's absolute dependence on God for salvation is made clear in the bestowal of redemption in a way that is "sensible." "Because we are first sinful, and utterly polluted, and afterward holy: so the production of the effect is sensible, and its derivation from God more obvious."[30] If we are first miserable and afterward happy, then the change is sensible. If we are first odious and afterward excellent, the change is sensibly observable. This change comes to us through the avenue of faith, for "there is included in the nature of faith, a sensibleness, and acknowledgement of this absolute dependence on God in this affair." When redemption comes, it is entirely fitting that its recipients should be "sensible of, and acknowledge the dependence on God for it."[31]

Edwards, in fact, on this occasion defines faith in terms of sensibility. "Faith is a sensibleness of what is real in the work of redemption; and as

28. *WJE* 14:204–5.
29. *WJE* 14:206.
30. *SJE* 71.
31. *SJE* 81.

we do really wholly depend on God, so the soul that believes doth entirely depend on God for all salvation, in its own sense, and act." To have saving faith, one must be "sensible that he is 'wretched, and miserable, and poor, and blind, and naked.' " The alteration from that position as a matter of the sovereign pleasure and power of God should be experienced with the same degree of sensibility. We must endeavor, therefore, to increase "in a sensibility of our great dependence on God, to have our eye to him alone, to mortify a self-dependent, and self-righteous disposition."[32]

In a sermon titled "The Reality of Conversion," Edwards gives reasons why conversion involves the granting of a new sense. He argues that it requires "something above nature to make a man love an unseen object so as cheerfully to lose all things and suffer all things for his sake." Natural sense works to cause people to "have a strong love to an object they have seen with their bodily eyes and have conversed with," but nature does not allow a love and devotion to an object that is remote to our present senses. Hearing of such a being as Jesus might cause "transient affections about that which they are so informed of," but does not "knit the heart so strongly to an unseen object" as to have the effect of insuperable devotion, love, and a willingness to lose this life for its sake. There must be, therefore, such a thing as conversion that gives a change of nature to produce "these new feelings of a sense of divine things." This new sense inhabits their natures in such a constituent manner so as "never wholly to leave them."[33]

When Edwards preached to the Mohawks, he used the language of the senses to communicate the kind of knowledge they needed to have if they truly were to come to Christ. In extrapolating both instruction and exhortation from the image of light in 2 Corinthians 4, Edwards assured them that "there is such a thing as this light's shining into the heart," and when it does so "it changes their hearts and makes 'em like to Jesus Christ." Just like true sunlight will make a glass shine and reflect the sun's brilliance and give a pleasant vision of a beautiful flower in the spring, so "when the light of God's word shines into the heart, it gives new life to the soul." As

---

32. *SJE* 80–81.
33. *SJE* 89, 91.

the sun shining on earth gives life to the trees, makes the earth look green, and causes flowers to appear and "give a good smell," so the light of God's word, shining in the heart, is "better than silver or gold" and is "sweeter than the honey." The gospel will "be a pleasant sound to you when you come to understand it." They should put themselves in the way of receiving this light, for if they never had this light shine in their hearts, they would have to dwell forever with the prince of darkness in the darkness of hell.[34]

Edwards focuses particularly on the reality of sight and how seeing and not seeing make the difference between salvation and damnation, heaven and hell. Those who do not believe in Christ and do not come to him for salvation have never seen how "excellent Christ is." For those who believe, however, "God opens their eyes to see how great and how glorious he is, and how good and how lovely he is." They see "the excellency of the great things that the Word of God teaches about Christ and the way of being saved by Him." Also, they "see what wicked miserable creatures they be, and so they see their need of a Savior to deliver from this misery." They come to Christ because "they see that they can't help themselves," and they "see how exceeding sinful they be, all over sinful, and that they deserve to be damned." If one merely hears these words and "don't see how wicked they be, and how they deserve to perish, can't come with all their hearts to Christ to save 'em."[35]

In his application, Edwards asks,

> Have your eyes ever been opened to see the glorious excellence of Jesus Christ? Has the light of the Word of God ever shined into your heart so that to see the excellence of the Word that teaches Christ and the work of salvation by him? Has that Word been made sweeter to you than the honey and honeycomb? Is the Word of Christ sweet food to your soul, that puts new life into you and is better than silver and gold?

---

34. *SJE* 109–10.
35. *SJE* 113.

Again, he asks what they see about their sin and their wickedness, what filthy, vile, and abominable creatures they are, and that they are "like a poor little infant that can't help yourself."[36]

Edwards also uses the word "sensible" on some occasions when he wants to emphasize the depth, insight, and feeling that a merely natural man could have of a truth even apart from his heart having been brought to love the truth. He makes this point clearly in "A Divine and Supernatural Light." Natural men may have "convictions of the guilt that lies upon them, and of the anger of God, and their danger of divine vengeance." These convictions are from "sensibleness of truth" and arise when some have "more light, or more of an apprehension of truth than others." But this kind of sensibility is a mere natural and keen awareness that comes from the Spirit's assisting the natural principles that are present in all people. Under the power of intense perceptions due to a combination of conscience and reason, an unregenerate person can become "sensible of guilt" and will find himself accused and condemned by conscience.

In this kind of sensibility, the Spirit works on the natural faculties of the person. In those who are born again, however, the Spirit communicates himself in his very nature to the person. He establishes a holy affection as a continued course of life by indwelling the person, operating *in* the person, not just *on* the person. He exerts his own nature in an actual alteration of mind and conscience. This operation is not merely on the imagination, nor is it the granting of new revelation or new truths not already contained in Scripture. Rather, the Spirit gives "a true sense of the divine excellency of the things revealed in the Word of God, and a conviction of the truth and reality of them, thence arising."[37]

In rapid succession, Edwards emphasizes the quality of this true, or real, "sense and apprehension of the divine excellency of things revealed in the Word of God." These include a "true sense of the divine and superlative excellency of the things of religion; a real sense of the excellency of God, and Jesus Christ, and of the work of redemption, and the ways and works of

---

36. *SJE* 118–19.
37. *SJE* 126.

God revealed in the gospel." This sense imbibes the "divine and superlative glory in these things; an excellency that is of a vastly higher kind, and more sublime nature, than in other things." The person made sensible by the Spirit operating in him sees "a glory greatly distinguishing them from all that is earthly and temporal. He that is spiritually enlightened truly apprehends and sees it, or has a sense of it." He not only rationally believes in the superlative glory of God, "but he has a sense of the gloriousness of God in his heart." Not only does he know rationally that God is holy and that holiness is a good thing, but "there is a sense of the loveliness of God's holiness." One may judge speculatively that God is gracious, but the spiritual person possesses "a sense how amiable God is upon that account; or a sense of the beauty of this divine attribute." This goes far beyond mere cognitive understanding, but "consists in the sense of the heart: as when there is a sense of the beauty, amiableness, or sweetness of a thing; so that the heart is sensible of pleasure and delight in the presence of the idea of it." In the one appears the best judgments of the speculative faculty, but in the other one finds "the will or disposition of the soul." The opinion that God is holy and gracious and "having a sense of the loveliness and beauty of that holiness and grace" is the difference between life and death.[38]

Returning to his propensity for taste and the uniqueness of the flavor of honey, Edwards reiterates, "There is a difference between having a rational judgment that honey is sweet, and having a sense of its sweetness."[39] One may have a rational judgment about the taste of honey from a variety of descriptions one has read or heard but be a total stranger to its real beauty and the impact it has on the senses, for one never has tasted it. One may have speculations about the nature of beauty, and be able to discuss philosophically the traits of the beautiful, but have no real knowledge of its expression in a particular instance, and the impact of that singular expression, until the beautiful thing itself is seen. "When the heart is sensible of the beauty and amiableness of a thing, it necessarily feels pleasure in the apprehension." Such pleasure in beauty is "implied in a person's being

---

38. *SJE* 127.
39. *SJE* 127.

heartily sensible of the loveliness of a thing, that the idea of it is sweet and pleasant to his soul."

The "sense of divine excellency of the things contained in the word of God" comes both indirectly and directly. Indirectly, such sensibility removes the prejudices against the superlative character of the issues prominent in the Bible and also aids the reason in its contemplation on the various and entertaining connections that tie together to holy doctrines of Scripture. Directly, however, by such a sensing of these matters of divine revelation, there is "an actual and lively discovery of this beauty and excellency." Such an experience will not allow one to reason that these things are merely human, or are fabulous without true substance, or can be subdued in their verity to ideas of lesser glory. Those who are sensible possess a "kind of intuitive and immediate evidence." Without this, true faith cannot arise. "Such a conviction of the truth of religion as this, arising, these ways, from a sense of the divine excellency of them, is that true spiritual conviction that there is in saving faith."[40] Or as he states it in another way, "This light, and this only, will bring the soul to a saving close with Christ."[41]

This sense of the intrinsic loveliness of Christ and all that the Bible reveals about him cannot come apart from the mind's cognition of those revealed propositions. The mind must be in possession of them for them to come to appear as beautiful and excellent. The sense of their divine excellency, however, comes only by the work of the Holy Spirit, and nothing else is either a proper or a mediate cause of this. "The mind can't see the excellency of any doctrine, unless that doctrine be first in the mind; but the seeing the excellency of the doctrine may be immediately from the Spirit of God."[42] The notions given to the mind come from one's natural comprehension of the nature of linguistic communication as presented in Scripture; the "due sense of the heart" is immediately from the Spirit. Reason's work is to perceive the truth, not to sense the beauty, loveliness, or excellency of anything.

---

40. *SJE* 129.
41. *SJE* 139.
42. *SJE* 131.

Edwards sets forth one of the most extensive investigations of the nature and desirability of assurance of salvation in his sermon "I Know That My Redeemer Liveth." After giving a display of the implied content of such knowledge, he shows the advantages that it gives to the traveler in this world, showing the many advantages of being able to say with confidence, "I know that my redeemer liveth." The first reason that he gives for his doctrine is the sensible experience of coming to a knowledge of all the glories of a Redeemer. "He sees in him that glory and excellency that is delightful and ravishing. That beauty is so great, so divine, that the sight of it, when it is so clearly seen, is above [all] things sweet. It fills the soul with a light so divine and powerful that it is impossible but the soul should be withal filled with peace and pleasantness. A sinking dullness and sorrow is not consistent with such bright light."[43] One's sensibility that one's Redeemer lives constitutes a major element of assurance.

Edwards, in fact, uses the term "sensible" of the experiential knowledge that Christ had of the implications of his own humanity. "None ever was so sensible of the distance between God and him, or had a heart so lowly before God, as the man Christ Jesus" (Matt 11:29). In his perfect humanity, Jesus discerned with perfection the virtually infinite distance there is between the glory of the uncreated and the created, the infinite and the finite, the eternal and the temporal. In his one person, he partook of both sides of these dichotomies and so dwelt with an infallible consciousness and spiritually sensory knowledge of these distinctions. In light of that, never has there been a man as genuinely humble, meek, reverent, patient, obedient, resigned, and dependent as Jesus of Nazareth. Not only was this perfectly clear as a matter of pure cognition with him, but it was a perfect, indelible, and immutable imprint on his affections and intrinsic to every perception of the beauty and excellence of the divine nature. As a corollary to that, the mere mortal who comes to something of a similar persuasion will share that sensibility; "because he that loves God is sensible in the hatefulness and vileness of sin committed against the being that he loves. And discerning an abundance of

---

43. *SJE* 148.

this in himself, he abhors himself in his own eyes, as unworthy of any good, and deserving of all evil."[44]

The sensibility of God's beauty as experienced in this world will unfold for the elect into a truly palpable sensate experience of the beauty of God. It is for this that God has made us and unto this end that he created the world. "So that 'tis evident that God made man to be happy in the beholding of God's own excellency," Edwards argues, "and seeing this is the end of man, doubtless this end shall be obtained to the full." What is the full attainment of this divinely conceived end? "There will be a time wherein man will, with open face and with as full a view as his nature is capable of, behold the excellency and beauty of God." This is no exhaustible experience, or one that diminishes and wanes in enjoyment with its continuance, for "seeing God's excellency is so great, even infinite, there is no doubt but the happiness in beholding it will be inconceivably great, even worthy of the gloriousness of the object." This journey of eternity will certainly be a "vast and unspeakable delight," a "very great blessedness" and a "very great felicity."[45]

Again, the relation of cognition and sensibility informs Edwards's argument in a sermon on Matthew 13:23, the parable of the sower. To get to the point of the fruitfulness of true faith, Edwards conflates cognition and sensibility more quickly than he does in other contexts, though both ideas still are present: "The understanding consists in the apprehension and judgment. And in order to the understanding of God's word, it is necessary that they should have a sensible and clear apprehension of the main things that are therein revealed, and that they should believe them." Such a "sensible apprehension" Edwards relates to the "glory of God," manifest in "the excellency and fullness of Christ which is taught in the Word" producing "the way of salvation" (focusing on Christ as the only person who could make a satisfying substitutionary atonement), and "the foundation of duty" (in the infinite majesty and excellence of God and the image of God in humanity). One grasps these essential revelatory and redemptive truths only

---

44. Jonathan Edwards, *Charity and Its Fruits* (Marshallton, DE: National Foundation for Christian Education, n.d.), 39.

45. *WJE* 14:147, 151.

when "God opens the eyes of his people to see these things." In this way one comes to have an "experimental knowledge of the nature of holiness which is recommended and required by the Word."[46]

Edwards gives a fascinating and graphic synonym for the concept of sensibility as he massages the meaning for memorable and convincing images. He observes, "But the faith of the godly, whereby they believe the Word of God to be true, is from the intrinsic signatures of divinity which they see in it." He preached on signatures of divine majesty, divine wisdom, divine holiness, and divine grace that "make it evident" that these ideas arise from what is certainly the word of God.

> God opens the understandings of profitable hearers to see these signatures and manifestations of divinity, so that they hear it as the Word of God. They do as it were hear God speak, and they are assured of the divinity of his speech, for he speaks like a God. His speech is not like the speech of men, but like the speech of God: divinely excellent, holy, wise, awful and gracious.
>
> And 'tis this sort of faith only that will hold the mind through all temptations. This is a sure foundation. This makes the truth of the gospel in a manner intuitively certain. When all other kinds of belief are wavering and unstable, this is an everlasting foundation.[47]

The sixth sense of Jonathan Edwards is one that all true believers share.

---

46. *WJE* 14:249–51.
47. *WJE* 14:252.

"FREE AND FRIENDLY COMMUNICATION OF OUR THOUGHTS"

The Friendship of Andrew Fuller and Thomas Steevens

MICHAEL A. G. HAYKIN

In the fall of 1799, William Wales Horne (1773–1826), the minister of the Baptist cause in Great Yarmouth, east Norfolk, gave two addresses that were later published together as a pamphlet titled *The Faith of the Gospel Vindicated* (1800). Part of the pamphlet attacks the idea that "Evangelical faith ... [is] the duty of the unconverted." As Horne goes on to argue, "If faith is the work of the Spirit, and at the same time the duty of the creature, it consequently follows, that it is the duty of a man dead in sin, to give himself the Spirit of God! A sentiment equally as absurd as presumptuous! and to be detested by all sincere advocates for the glory of free grace!"[1] In other words, Horne denies the free offer of the gospel to all and sundry.[2] Not surprisingly, when this pamphlet fell into the hands of that day's most ardent

---

1. William Wales Horne, *The Faith of the Gospel Vindicated: Being the Substance of Two Sermons, Delivered Extempore at the Baptist Meeting, Great Yarmouth, Oct. 27, 1799* (Yarmouth, UK, 1800), 33.

2. Horne, *Faith of the Gospel Vindicated*, 26–27. Elsewhere, Horne claims to be a defender of "repentance toward God, and faith toward our Lord Jesus Christ, as covenant blessings, the free gifts of Jehovah, and of the operation of the Holy Spirit in the souls of the redeemed, against the duty faith men, or Semi-arminians." See Horne, *Biblical Criticisms and Illustrations of Experimental Godliness, The Solutions to Critical Questions in Theology* (London: W. Day, 1825), vi.

defender of the affirmation that faith is indeed the duty of all to whom the gospel comes, namely, Andrew Fuller (1754–1815), minister of the Baptist work in Kettering, Northamptonshire, he fired off a small piece that has been transmitted under the title "Remarks on Two Sermons by W. W. Horne of Yarmouth."[3] Among other things, Fuller was distressed that Horne had used the pulpit to launch an attack on those who, like him, held to the free offer of the gospel. As he says:

> It is not by converting the pulpit into a stage of strife, nor by availing ourselves of the silence which decency imposes upon an audience to pour forth personal invective, that truth is promoted. ... It is by reading, by calm and serious reflection, by humble prayer, and by a free and friendly communication of our thoughts to one another in private conversation, that truth makes progress.[4]

In these occasional remarks, Fuller reveals a fundamental aspect of his thinking about right and wrong ways to promote biblical truth. Truth was to be promoted through what historically has been called the means of grace. Fuller mentions four in this text: reflective reading, meditation on what has been read, prayer, and personal conversations. It could be demonstrated quite easily that all of these means mentioned were part of Fuller's own way of appropriating and disseminating truth and piety.[5] The final one—"free and friendly communication of our thoughts to one another in private

---

3. Andrew Fuller, "Remarks on Two Sermons by W. W. Horne of Yarmouth," in *The Complete Works of the Rev. Andrew Fuller*, 1845 ed. (repr., Harrisonburg, VA: Sprinkle, 1988), 3:578–85. Horne subsequently replied to Fuller with his *A Scriptural Defence of the Truth, As it is in Jesus* (Nottingham, UK: J. Plumbe, 1801) and sarcastically referred to him as "a great master in Baptist Israel."

4. Fuller, "Remarks on Two Sermons," 582.

5. See the references to Fuller in Michael A. G. Haykin, "'Draw Nigh unto my Soul': English Baptist Piety and the Means of Grace in the Seventeenth and Eighteenth Centuries," *The Southern Baptist Journal of Theology* 10, no.4 (Winter 2006): 54–73. See also Nathan A. Finn, "Andrew Fuller's Edwardsean Spirituality," in *The Pure Flame of Devotion: The History of Christian Spirituality; Essays in Honour of Michael A. G. Haykin*, ed. G. Stephen Weaver and Ian Hugh Clary (Kitchener, ON: Joshua, 2013), 383–404.

conversation"—is especially noteworthy, for this is a means of grace that has been frequently overlooked in twentieth-century reflection on Christian piety.[6]

Fuller was blessed to be part of a close-knit circle of friends, including missionary William Carey (1761–1834), John Sutcliff of Olney (1754–1815), and John Ryland Jr. (1753–1825), Fuller's first biographer and the principal of Bristol Baptist Academy.[7] Fuller thus knew from personal experience how vital it was to sit down with such men and talk through issues. In fact, such discussions took place when Fuller and other ministers of the Northamptonshire Association met regularly for prayer and fellowship.

"THE REVIVAL OF REAL RELIGION"

On April 23, 1784, for instance, John Ryland received in the mail a treatise by Jonathan Edwards (1703–58), the "greatest Christian theologian of the eighteenth century,"[8] dealing with corporate prayer and revival, which had been sent to him by Scottish Presbyterian minister John Erskine (1721–1803). When Erskine was in his mid-twenties he had entered into regular correspondence with Edwards and had become part of a close-knit letter-writing network of Scottish, English, and American ministers committed to the promotion of the evangelical revival. Long after Edwards's death in 1758, Erskine continued to uphold the theological perspectives of this network of ministers and to recommend heartily books that they had written, especially those by Edwards.

Well described as "the paradigm of Scottish evangelical missionary interest through the last half of the eighteenth century,"[9] Erskine regularly

---

6. See the argument of Joanne J. Jung, *The Lost Discipline of Conversation: Surprising Lessons in Spiritual Formation Drawn from the English Puritans* (Grand Rapids: Zondervan, 2018).

7. On these friendships, see Michael A. G. Haykin, *One Heart and One Soul: John Sutcliff of Olney, His Friends, and His Times* (Darlington, UK: Evangelical Press, 1994); and Haykin, *Ardent Love to Jesus: English Baptists and the Experience of Revival in the Long Eighteenth Century* (Bryntirion, UK: Bryntirion, 2013).

8. Miklós Vetö, "Book Reviews: *America's Theologian. A Recommendation of Jonathan Edwards. By Robert W. Jenson,*" *Church History* 58 (1989): 522.

9. J. A. De Jong, *As the Waters Cover the Sea. Millennial Expectations in the Rise of Anglo-American Missions 1640–1810* (Kampen, The Netherlands: Kok, 1970), 166. On Erskine, see the excellent

corresponded with both Sutcliff and Ryland from 1780 until his death in 1803, sending them not only letters but also on occasion bundles of interesting books and tracts he was seeking to promote.[10] Thus it was in mid-April 1784 that Erskine mailed to Ryland a copy of Edwards's *An Humble Attempt to Promote Explicit Agreement and Visible Union of God's People in Extraordinary Prayer for the Revival of Religion and the Advancement of Christ's Kingdom on Earth, pursuant to Scripture Promises and Prophecies concerning the Last Time*. Knowing the affection that Sutcliff and Fuller had for Edwards's writings, Ryland lost no time in sharing this treatise with his two friends.

Edwards's treatise was inspired by a transatlantic movement of regular prayer meetings for revival that had sprung up in the early 1740s. In it, Edwards argues that preceding all times of regular revival were regular, corporate meetings, what he called "concerts," of Christians praying for revival and God's advance of his church. Reading Edwards's *Humble Attempt* in the final week of April 1784 evidently had a profound impact on Ryland. He immediately shared it with Fuller and Sutcliff, on whom it had a similar effect. The following month, after they had read Edwards's treatise and discussed its implications for their own historical context, these three Baptist pastors, together with a few other ministerial colleagues, committed themselves to meeting the second Tuesday in every other month "to seek the revival of real religion, and the extension of Christ's kingdom in the world."[11] A few weeks later, the Northamptonshire Association of Baptist churches, to which the three friends and their respective churches belonged, issued what has come to be called the Prayer Call of 1784, which was one of the key harbingers of widespread revival among the transatlantic Baptist community. Among other things, the Prayer Call, as written by Sutcliff, states that "the grand object of prayer is to be that the Holy Spirit may be poured

study by Jonathan M. Yeager, *Enlightened Evangelicalism: The Life and Thought of John Erskine* (Oxford: Oxford University Press, 2011).

10. For an extant piece of Erskine's correspondence with Sutcliff, see John Erskine, Letter to John Sutcliff, October 14, 1799 (The Isaac Mann Collection, The James Marshall and Marie-Louise Osborn Collection, Yale University Library, New Haven). For other details of Erskine's correspondence with Sutcliff and Ryland, see Yeager, *Enlightened Evangelicalism*, passim.

11. John Ryland Jr., *The Work of Faith, the Labour of Love, and the Patience of Hope, illustrated; in the Life and Death of the Reverend Andrew Fuller* (London: Button & Son, 1816), 150.

down on our ministers and churches, that sinners may be converted, the interest of religion revived, and the name of God glorified."[12]

"SUCH LIVES AS BRAINERD AND EDWARDS"

This combination of praying and reading together among Fuller and his friends is well captured by an entry in the diary of John Ryland, where he noted that on January 21, 1788:

> Brethren, Fuller, Sutcliff, Carey, and I, kept this day as a private fast in my study: read the Epistles to Timothy and Titus; Booth's Charge to Hopkins; Blackerby's Life, in Gillies; and Rogers of Dedham's Sixty Memorials for a Godly Life: and each prayed twice—Carey with singular enlargement and pungency. Our chief design was to implore a revival of the power of godliness in our own souls, in our churches, and in the church at large.[13]

Three specific works beyond the apostle Paul's Pastoral Epistles are mentioned here. First there was the classic ministerial charge by Abraham Booth (1734–1806) to Thomas Hopkins (1759–87), known as *Pastoral Cautions* (1785).[14] Booth filled the pulpit for nearly forty years of one of the most prestigious London churches, Little Prescot Street Baptist Church, in what was then a wealthy area of London, home to merchants and professional men. As a theologian, he stood high in the regard of Fuller and his circle of friends, and indeed in the esteem of their entire denomination. In 1808, two years after Booth had died, Fuller publicly praised Booth as "the first counsellor of our denomination."[15] Earlier, while Booth was still living,

---

12. John Sutcliff, "The Prayer Call of 1784," in *The Nature, Evidences, and Advantages, of Humility*, by John Ryland Jr. (Circular Letter of the Northamptonshire Association, 1784), 12. For a detailed discussion of this call to prayer and its historical context, see Haykin, *One Heart and One Soul*, 153–71.

13. Cited in J. E. Ryland, "Memoir," in *Pastoral Memorials: Selected from the Manuscripts of the Late Rev. John Ryland, D.D. of Bristol*, ed. J. E. Ryland (London: B. J. Holdsworth, 1826), 1:17n.

14. See Michael A. G. Haykin with Alison E. Haykin, eds., *The Works of Abraham Booth* (Springfield, MO: Particular Baptist, 2006), 1:57–84.

15. Cited in Ernest A. Payne, "Abraham Booth, 1734–1806," *BQ* 26 (1975–76): 28.

Benjamin Beddome (1718–95), one of the most significant Baptist hymn writers of the era, exclaimed, "Oh, that Abraham Booth's God may be my God."[16] The other works that Fuller and his circle of friends read were both Puritan: the life of Richard Blackerby (1574–1648), which was published in John Gillies's *Historical Collections Relating to Remarkable Periods of the Success of the Gospel, and Eminent Instruments Employed in Promoting It* (1754), and *Sixty Memorials of a Godly Life*, frequently assigned to John Rogers of Dedham (d. 1636), a fiery Puritan preacher.[17] Presumably the friends discussed the content of what they read and in this way sought to enflame their hearts and strengthen their wills in God's service.

There is further evidence from the writings of Fuller and his friends that especially the works of John Owen (1616–83), regarded by some fellow Puritans as the "Calvin of England," and Jonathan Edwards were also being deeply read and discussed by this "band of brothers."[18] To take but one example: in the summer of 1793, Fuller wrote to Thomas Steevens (1745–1802), the pastor of Colchester Baptist Church, Essex, from 1774 until his death, that when he read about "such lives as Brainerd and Edwards, I am utterly ashamed of my own."[19] Fuller is referencing here the life of David Brainerd (1718–47) that had been written by Edwards shortly after the

---

16. Cited in John Rippon, *A Short Memoir of the Rev. Abraham Booth*, in James Dore, *A Sermon, occasioned by the Death of The Rev. Abraham Booth, Preached in Little Prescot Street, Goodman's Fields … : And A Short Memoir of the Deceased, incorporated with The Address Delivered at his Interment … by John Rippon* (London, 1806), 85n.

17. For a brief review of Rogers's character and ministry, see Michael A. G. Haykin, "A Boanerges and a Barnabas," *Tabletalk* 36, no.3 (March 2012): 32–33.

18. See, for example, Carl Trueman, "John Owen and Andrew Fuller," *Eusebeia* 9 (2008): 53–69; Shane Shaddix, "'In Exhortation, Invitations, Precepts, and Threatenings': Andrew Fuller, John Owen, and the Free Offer of the Gospel," in *Understanding Andrew Fuller: Life, Thought, and Legacies*, ed. Nathan A. Finn, Shane Shaddix, and C. Jeffrey Robinson Sr. (Eugene, OR: Pickwick, forthcoming); Chris Chun, "'Sense of the Heart': Jonathan Edwards' Legacy in the Writings of Andrew Fuller," *Eusebeia* 9 (2008): 117–34; Chun, *The Legacy of Jonathan Edwards in the Theology of Andrew Fuller*, Studies in the History of Christian Traditions 162 (Leiden: Brill, 2012). On Owen as the Calvin of England, see Allen C. Guelzo, "John Owen, Puritan Pacesetter," *Christianity Today* 20, no. 17 (May 1976): 14; Richard L. Greaves, "Owen, John (1616–1683)," in *Oxford Dictionary of National Biography*, online ed. (Oxford: Oxford University Press, 2004), https://doi-org.proxy1.lib.uwo.ca/10.1093/ref:odnb/21016.

19. Andrew Fuller, Letter to Thomas Steevens, July 8, 1793, in "Extracts from the Late Rev. A. Fuller's Correspondence with the Late Rev. Mr. Steevens, of Colchester," *The Baptist Magazine* 8 (1816): 494.

former's death, and Samuel Hopkins's (1721–1803) *The Life and Character of the Late Reverend, Learned, and Pious Mr. Jonathan Edwards* (1764), which Fuller possessed in a 1785 Glasgow edition.[20] Obviously he expected Steevens to be familiar with both biographies. Reflection on and discussion of Scripture and Christian literature thus deeply shaped and informed the lives of these Christian brothers.

"I ADMIRE THE SPIRIT OF THE AUTHOR"

When Fuller was unable to meet his friends face to face, he used the medium of the letter to convey the "free and friendly communication of [his] thoughts." The remainder of this essay will consider in this regard a slice of his correspondence with the Colchester pastor mentioned above, Thomas Steevens.[21] Born in Northamptonshire, Steevens's parents had sat under the powerful ministry of Congregationalist Philip Doddridge (1702–51). Another leading influence on him in his early years was the elder John Ryland (1723–91), pastor of the open-communion Baptist church in Northampton and the somewhat eccentric father of Fuller's friend of the same name. Steevens himself was baptized as a believer in July 1771 by John Macgowan (1726–80) at Devonshire Square Baptist Church in London, and two years later called by this church to a preaching ministry.[22]

His first and only pastoral charge was over the Eld Lane congregation of Baptists in Colchester, where he began to preach in January of 1774 and to which he was formally called as pastor in May of that year. Despite

---

20. For Fuller's possession of these books, see "Books in Fuller's Library, 1798," in *The Diary of Andrew Fuller, 1780–1801*, ed. Michael D. McMullen and Timothy D. Whelan, The Complete Works of Andrew Fuller 1 (Berlin: de Gruyter, 2016), 221.

21. For his life, see "Memoir of the Rev. Thomas Steevens," *The Baptist Magazine* 9 (1817): 81–88.

22. "Memoir of the Rev. Thomas Steevens," 83; Henry Spyvee, *Colchester Baptist Church—The First 300 Years, 1689–1989* (Colchester: Colchester Baptist Church, 1989), 31. Spyvee calls the London pastor "Joseph Macgowan." The anonymous memoir from *The Baptist Magazine* places Steevens's baptism in 1772, though Timothy Whelan places it in 1771. See Whelan, "Biographical Index of Dissenters, 1700–1860," https://sites.google.com/a/georgiasouthern.edu/tim-whelan/dissenting-studies/biographical-index-dissenters-1700-1860 (accessed August 5, 2018). On Macgowan, see Charlotte Fell-Smith, Rev. J. H. Y. Briggs, "Macgowan, John (1726–1780)," in *Oxford Dictionary of National Biography*, https://doi-org.proxy1.lib.uwo.ca/10.1093/ref:odnb/17516.

the fact that the congregation was characterized by a contentious spirit from time to time, Steevens had a highly successful ministry.[23] Some 169 people were baptized during his pastorate and came into the membership of the congregation, which had to double the size of the church building to accommodate all of the congregants.[24] Steevens also played a key role in the formation of the Essex Baptist Association at Coggeshall in 1796,[25] and he was an ardent advocate of the cause of foreign missions, which endeared him to Fuller.

The first extant contact of the Fuller circle of friends with Steevens appears to be a letter that Steevens wrote to John Sutcliff on November 10, 1785, and which Sutcliff received three weeks later. Steevens had read Fuller's *The Gospel of Christ Worthy of All Acceptation*, which had appeared earlier in 1785, and was convinced that he and Fuller shared much theologically:

> You wish to know my thoughts of that gentlemans [i.e.,
> Fuller] publication—I will be perfectly free, however much
> I may prove myself precipitate & even ignorant in what I
> wrote before.—I admire the Spirit of the author—it appears
> plain I think that his alone wish is to propagate Truth—I
> admire the perspicuity of his manner which conveys at once
> his meaning to the mind—Nor can I find anything to say
> against, but much to say for the Sentiment. I was rather
> averse to it before, either because I did not understand it,

23. Spyvee, *Colchester Baptist Church*, 32; Janet Cooper and W. R. Powell, "Protestant Nonconformity," in *A History of the County of Essex*, vol. 9, *The Borough of Colchester*, ed. Janet Cooper (Oxford: The Institute of Historical Research by Oxford University Press, 1994), 340–41. In 1785, Steevens told John Sutcliff that some of his congregation were complaining that he was "wishing them to be more holy than God requires"! See Thomas Steevens, Letter to John Sutcliff, November 10, 1785, in *Baptist Autographs in the John Rylands University Library of Manchester, 1741–1845*, transcribed and ed. Timothy Whelan (Macon, GA: Mercer University Press, 2009), 48.

24. "Memoir of the Rev. Thomas Steevens," 85.

25. Steevens preached his sermon "The Knowledge of God Increased, and His Church Enlarged" (London, 1796) at the founding of the Association. He also spoke the following year at the association's first anniversary, which was held in the Congregationalist Church in Coggeshall. See George Frederick Beaumont, *A History of Coggeshall, in Essex* (London: Marshall Brothers/Coggeshall: Edwin Potter, 1890), 149.

or because it was wrongly stated by others—the last I think
was the chief reason; for I now recollect, that for seven years
past & more I have been coming over to his mind tho' I did
not know, that I had any Partners—thinking upon that text
with a view to the pulpit "ye will not come to me that you
may have Life" [John 5:40] led me into a quite (for me) new
train of Thought upon mans Inability & I found and said it
lies in his will. … It appears to me that M^r F[uller] deserves
the thanks of all the Lovers of simple Truth.[26]

Fuller's book was designed to affirm both divine sovereignty in the salvation
of sinners and human responsibility to respond to the gospel proclamation.[27]
And although Steevens, in the early stages of his ministry in Colchester,
would have found fault with Fuller's theology, by the time that he read *The
Gospel of Christ Worthy of All Acceptation* he realized that his own theological
development paralleled that of Fuller.

Yet there were many known to Steevens who were firm in their refusal to
see Fuller's theology as anything but a variant of Arminianism. As Steevens
told Sutcliff:

It pleases me, that some very sensible Independents here
about have the Book [of Fuller] and esteem it—But my
baptist Brethren will not receive it & some of them already
deem me an Arminian for only attempting to explain to them
the meaning of the phrases moral & natural Inability—I

---

26. Steevens, Letter to Sutcliff, November 10, 1785, in Whelan, *Baptist Autographs*, 47
(spelling original). For the entire letter, see 46–48.

27. See the discussion by Keith S. Grant, *Andrew Fuller and the Evangelical Renewal of Pastoral
Theology*, Studies in Baptist History and Thought 36 (Milton Keynes, UK: Paternoster, 2013),
45–49; Peter J. Morden, "Andrew Fuller and the Birth of 'Fullerism,' " *BQ* 46 (2015): 139–52;
and Michael A. G. Haykin, "A Historical and Biblical Root of the Globalization of Christianity:
The Fullerism of Andrew Fuller's *The Gospel Worthy of All Acceptation*," *Puritan Reformed Journal*
8 (January 2016): 165–76. For Fuller's confidence in God's sovereignty in the conversion of
sinners, see his Letter to Thomas Steevens, April 14, 1795, in "Extracts from the Late Rev. A.
Fuller's Correspondence," 495: "Men's hearts there [in India], are the same as here; nothing
short of an Almighty arm, will pull down the strong holds of error and superstition."

have had some warm, I don't mean angry, disputes upon
the Subject.[28]

The counties of Suffolk and Norfolk, to the immediate north of Steevens's
church in Colchester, were a bastion of high Calvinism.[29] Witness William
Wales Horne, the critic of Fuller with whom this essay began.[30] In fact, the
term "Fullerism" may well have originated in this locale. Norfolk Baptist
pastor Job Hupton (1762–1849), for example, employed this term as early
as 1803 in a pamphlet to denote specifically the concept, erroneous in his
mind, that it is "the duty of all who hear the gospel to believe it." In this pithy
phrase, Hupton accurately caught an essential aspect of Fuller's thinking,
though the same cannot be said for his further critique of Fuller's theology
as that of a "buffoon" who regarded all "who cannot swallow his sophisms,
or subscribe to his creed, as if they were not worthy to black his shoes."[31]

Fuller's response to Hupton's pamphlet was an 1804 book review in
which he comments:

> To call the principles opposed in this piece [by Hupton]
> *Fullerism* … shows but little acquaintance with things. If the
> doctrine which Mr. Fuller has defended contained any thing
> new, or different from what has been taught by all our divines,
> except a few in the last century, there might have been some
> colour for giving it a new name. But it does not: and therefore

---

28. Steevens, Letter to Sutcliff, November 10, 1785, in Whelan, *Baptist Autographs*, 47.
Spelling original.

29. For the term "high Calvinism" rather than "hyper-Calvinism," see Geoffrey F. Nuttall,
"Northamptonshire and the Modern Question: A Turning-Point in Eighteenth-Century Dissent,"
in *Studies in English Dissent* (Weston Rhyn, UK: Quinta, 2002), 207 and n. 4. Fuller himself
uses the term "High Calvinist" in his letters to Steevens: see Andrew Fuller, Letter to Thomas
Steevens, June 19, 1795, in "Extracts from the Late Rev. A. Fuller's Correspondence," 495–96.

30. See also *A Testimony in Favour of the Principles Maintained by the Suffolk and Norfolk Association
of Particular Baptist Churches, on the Doctrines of Grace* (London: W. Button, 1807), in which Fuller
and his theology are repeatedly and extensively attacked by name (pp. 3, 9, 13–14, 20–23).
Fuller is criticized for erecting "a stately fabric of creature-holiness and mere morality" (9), and
his argumentation likened to that characteristic of Arminian authors (14).

31. Job Hupton, "Preface," to *A Blow struck at the Root of Fullerism* (London: L. J. Higham,
1803), http://www.mountzionpbc.org/Duty%20Faith/Job_Hupton_Fullerism.pdf.

it might as well be called Calvinism, Owenism or Bunyanism, as Fullerism.[32]

Fuller was confident that his theology had much deeper roots in the Reformed tradition than his own reflections and theological struggles with high Calvinism.

"WE WISH TO DO SOMETHING MORE THAN PRAY"

The first extant letter of Fuller to Steevens comes from the spring of 1793, when Fuller sought to acquaint his fellow pastor with details regarding the progress of the Baptist Missionary Society, which Fuller and his friends had founded in 1792.[33] Fuller informed Steevens about the way that the Society had been led to appoint a surgeon named John Thomas (1757–1801) to accompany William Carey as a missionary to India.[34] During an earlier voyage to India in 1786 Thomas had become friends with Charles Grant (1746–1823), an Anglican evangelical who was on the board of trade of the powerful East India Company and who was based in Calcutta. Grant had helped Thomas to start a missionary enterprise in Bengal, where Thomas began to learn Bengali and to translate the Scriptures into that tongue, and also made some headway in learning Sanskrit. He was deeply moved by the wretchedness, both spiritual and material, of many of the Indian people and longed to alleviate it.

For a variety of reasons, not the least of which was a significant financial indebtedness and Thomas's mercurial temper, by 1790 the friendship between Thomas and Grant had soured to the point that Thomas had had to return to England in the early months of 1792 to secure a new source of funding to undergird his missionary work in Bengal. He also hoped to find, if at all possible, a like-minded companion for the work in India. Almost

---

32. Cited in J. W. Morris, *Memoirs of the Life and Writings of the Rev. Andrew Fuller*, rev. ed. (London: Wightman and Cramp, 1826), 238–39.

33. Andrew Fuller, Letter to Thomas Steevens [1793], in "Extracts from the Late Rev. A. Fuller's Correspondence," 452–53.

34. On Thomas, see Arthur C. Chute, *John Thomas, First Baptist Missionary to Bengal, 1757–1801* (Halifax, NS: Baptist Book and Tract Society, 1893); and Michael Whitfield, "Dr John Thomas: The First Baptist Missionary to Bengal," *BQ* 46 (2015): 153–65.

as soon as the ship had made landfall in England on July 8, Thomas got in touch with the London pastors Samuel Stennett (1727–1795) and Abraham Booth. He made known to them his desire with regard to a mission to India, and it was Booth who put Thomas into contact with Carey and Fuller. Booth told Fuller that he considered Thomas "a suitable person" to send with Carey.[35]

Steevens did not know Carey personally, but Fuller told him that he was "a noble creature, ready at learning languages; open, generous, and upright; ardent—of sound principles—a disinterested soul, and a heart that comprehends the welfare of a world." Fuller notes that "there were difficulties" in the path of the mission, but Carey was "formed on purpose to surmount difficulty."[36] Of course, key among these difficulties would have been the reluctance of Carey's wife, Dorothy Plackett Carey (1756–1807), to accompany her husband, though Fuller does not mention this specifically to Steevens.[37]

This mission to India, Fuller hastens to add, was not a matter of a few months' planning. It grew out of close to a decade of prayer: "We have not gone about this business in a hurry; we have been praying by monthly prayer-meetings for it these eight or nine years, and now we wish to do something more than pray."[38] This is a reference to the 1784 Prayer Call noted above, in which there was also a definite missionary focus. The Northamptonshire Baptists had been encouraged to pray that in addition to revival in the British Isles there would also be a spread of the gospel "to the most distant parts of the habitable globe."[39]

Fuller further notes that he and his friends in the Northamptonshire Association "have solemnly bound ourselves to God, and one another" to engage in supporting this mission "by individual subscriptions, and

---

35. Fuller, Letter to Steevens [1793], 452. For further detail regarding Fuller's decision to send Thomas with Carey, see Haykin, *One Heart and One Soul*, 225–27.

36. Fuller, Letter to Steevens [1793], 453.

37. See the very balanced account of Dorothy's life by James Beck, *Dorothy Carey: The Tragic and Untold Story of Mrs. William Carey* (repr., Eugene, OR: Wipf & Stock, 2000).

38. Fuller, Letter to Steevens [1793], 453.

39. Sutcliff, "Prayer Call of 1784," in Ryland Jr., *Nature, Evidences, and Advantages, of Humility*, 12.

congregational collections." Fuller communicates these details with the hope that Steevens and his Colchester church can help financially. "We exert ourselves to the utmost," Fuller comments, but at the same time "we rely upon God, trusting he will open the hearts of our brethren in every quarter of the kingdom, to assist in this good work." This combination of radical commitment and total trust in divine sovereignty is typically Fuller. Finally, the way that Fuller closes this initial letter to the Essex pastor augurs a deepening friendship: "I am, Dear Sir, your affectionate brother in our dear Lord."[40]

"SWEET AND SAVOURY PLEASANTRY"

None of Steevens's letters to Fuller appear to be extant. But he evidently replied to Fuller's first letter before Fuller wrote a second time on March 26, 1793. In this second letter Fuller is thrilled to tell Steevens that £800 had already been raised, though none of it had come from the wealthy Baptist congregations in London. There, far too many had followed the advice of Samuel Stennett, who urged extreme caution. "The mission," Fuller quotes him as saying, "will come to nothing from this cause—people may contribute … for once in a fit of zeal, but how is it to be [continually] supported?"[41] Fuller's response to Stennett's skepticism is to declare that his trust is not in human support and resources at all, but in God. As he tells Steevens:

> For my part, I believe in God, and have not much doubt but that a matter, begun as this was, will meet his approbation: and that he who has inclined the hearts of our brethren hitherto so much beyond our expectations, will go on to incline their hearts "not to lose the things which they have wrought" [2 John 1:8]. I confess I feel sanguine in my hopes, but they are fixed in God.[42]

---

40. Fuller, Letter to Steevens [1793], 453.

41. Andrew Fuller, Letter to Thomas Steevens, March 26, 1793, in "Extracts from the Late Rev. A. Fuller's Correspondence," 453.

42. Fuller, Letter to Steevens, March 26, 1793, in "Extracts from the Late Rev. A. Fuller's Correspondence," 453.

By the early nineteenth century, the Baptist Missionary Society was regularly receiving £3,000 or more a year.[43] Fuller's hope had not been misplaced.

In his closing remarks Fuller includes Zenas Trivett (d. 1831), the pastor of the Baptist cause in Langham, Essex, from 1778–1819: "My Christian love to Mr. Trivet, or any others you may think proper. A thousand thanks to you and him for your exertions. … If I were within a day's ride of you any time, I should be tempted to come and see you. … Grace be with you, so prays your affectionate, A. Fuller. Brother Ryland unites in love."[44] Although Fuller had not yet met Steevens face to face, the latter's warm advocacy of the missionary cause dear to Fuller's heart had quickened the latter's desire to meet him as well as the expressions of love he declared.[45]

The way in which the churches supporting the Baptist Missionary Society were bound together in love was the keynote of Fuller's next letter to Steevens, dated May 18, 1793:

> My dear brother,
>
>   I cannot but bless God for this business, in many points of view. One is, it introduces me to a more intimate

---

43. This may be readily seen by consulting the subscription lists contained in the *Periodical Accounts* issued by the Baptist Missionary Society during the first dozen years of the nineteenth century.

44. Fuller, Letter to Steevens, March 26, 1793, 454. Zenas Trivett was the youngest son of Edward Trivett (1712–92), the pastor of a thriving Baptist work in Worstead, Norfolk. Ten years after Trivett retired from Langham, the congregation numbered around 450, the bulk of whom had been added during Trivett's ministry. See Joseph Ivimey, *A History of the English Baptists* (London: Isaac Taylor Hinton and Holdsworth & Ball, 1830), 4:125, 524; "Obituary: Rev. Zenas Trivett," *The Baptist Magazine* 23 (1831): 537–38; Maurice F. Hewett, "Early Days at Worstead," *BQ* 11 (1942–45): 168–70. Proof that it was indeed Zenas Trivett is found in Andrew Fuller, Letter to Thomas Steevens, October 5, 1793, in "Extracts from the Late Rev. A. Fuller's Correspondence," 494, where Fuller mentions his visit to Langham. Trivett also preached Steevens's funeral sermon ("Memoir of the Rev. Thomas Steevens," 87). Sadly, there is no mention in the minute books of the Langham church of its early support of the Baptist Missionary Society. See J. E. Compton, "Colchester and the Missionary Movement," *BQ* 11 (1942–45): 55. The Baptist chapel in Langham closed around 1939. See Christopher Stell, *An Inventory of Nonconformist Chapels and Meeting-Houses in Eastern England* (Swindon, UK: English Heritage, 2002), 58.

45. For love as a key element in Fuller's understanding of pastoral practice, see Paul A. Sanchez, *The Spirituality of Love in Andrew Fuller's Ordination Sermons* (Louisville, KY: Andrew Fuller Center for Baptist Studies, 2018).

acquaintance with my brethren, whom, as I know, I dearly love. The names of Fawcett, and Crabtree, and Pearce, and Birt, and Steadman, and Steevens, and many more, are herby embalmed in my remembrance for ever.

I knew the opposition made to "Andrew Fuller," in S[uffolk] and N[orfolk], and though you may think me fond of fighting, I am too much a lover of peace and quietness, to embroil myself in unnecessary disputes, and which, in that case, I suppose, would be like a bear with his nose in a wasp's nest.

... O my dear brother, it would do your heart good to see the love to Christ, and the souls of men, discovered in many parts of the country, in readily contributing to this business. Good old Mr. Crabtree, of Bradford, in Yorkshire, upwards of seventy, could not sleep for joy: he laboured night and day, went to the vicar and curate, who cheerfully gave him a guinea each; obtained in the whole upwards of £40 and a great deal of respect from the neighbourhood into the account. "My heart has been so much in this work," says the venerable man, "that it has almost been too much for my poor old body." "Blessed be God," says dear Mr. Fawcett, of Brearly-hall, near Halifax, "that I have lived to see so much love to Christ. I account it one of the greatest blessings of my life, to have assisted in so glorious and disinterested an undertaking." Birt, of Plymouth-dock; Steadman, of Broughton, in Hampshire, and many more, write all in the same strain. I feel an exquisite satisfaction that we have made the attempt: the issue is in his hands, whose cause it is.[46]

The larger English Calvinistic Baptist community to which both Fuller and Steevens belonged did not have a national framework until the nineteenth

---

46. Andrew Fuller, Letter to Thomas Steevens, May 18, 1793, in "Extracts from the Late Rev. A. Fuller's Correspondence," 454.

century, but as this letter indicates, support for and engagement in overseas missions helped to unify and bring into loving contact Baptist causes throughout England. In addition to Steevens, five other Baptist leaders are mentioned here: John Fawcett (1740–1817) and William Crabtree (1720–1811), both pastoring in the West Riding of Yorkshire; Samuel Pearce (1766–99) of Birmingham; Isaiah Birt (1758–1837) of Plymouth; and William Steadman (1764–1837) from Broughton, Hampshire.[47] The cords of mission that bound Fuller to these men were not simply that, as Fuller emphasized. The mission was a vehicle that deepened Fuller's love for these men.

Commenting on the opposition to his theology in Norfolk and Suffolk, noted above, Fuller emphasizes that he is not at heart a lover of theological conflict, or as he puts it vividly, he has no desire to be like "a bear with his nose in a wasp's nest." And yet Fuller spent much of his life embroiled in theological battles.[48] First he debated with with the high Calvinists, as

47. John Fawcett (1740–1817) was an important influence for revival among the Yorkshire Baptists. On his life and ministry, see John Fawcett Jr., *An Account of the Life, Ministry, and Writings of the Late Rev. John Fawcett D.D.* (London: Baldwin, Cradock, and Joy/Halifax: P. K. Holden, 1818); Ian Sellers, "Other Times, Other Ministries: John Fawcett and Alexander McLaren," *BQ* 32 (1986–87): 181–99; Michael A. G. Haykin, *"Blest Be the Tie That Binds": Remembering John Fawcett; His Times, His Life, His Hymn* (Louisville, KY: Andrew Fuller Center for Baptist Studies, 2018). William Crabtree (1720–1811) was pastor of the Baptist cause in Bradford, Yorkshire, for fifty years. For his life and ministry, see Isaac Mann, *Memoirs of the Late Rev. Wm. Crabtree* (London: Button and Son, 1815). Samuel Pearce was one of Fuller's closest friends. Fuller wrote his memoir after Pearce's early death in 1799, which became the most printed work from Fuller's pen in the nineteenth century. See Andrew Fuller, *Memoirs Of the late Rev. Samuel Pearce, A. M.* (Clipstone: J. W. Morris, 1800). For Pearce's piety, see Haykin, *Joy Unspeakable and Full of Glory: The Piety of Samuel and Sarah Pearce* (Kitchener, ON: Joshua, 2012). Isaiah Birt (1758–1837) pastored Baptist churches at Plymouth Dock and in Birmingham. See John Birt, "Memoir of the Late Rev. Isaiah Birt," *The Baptist Magazine* 30 (1838): 54–59, 107–16, 197–203. William Steadman (1764–1837) pastored at Broughton, Hampshire, from 1791 to 1798. He assisted Birt at Plymouth Dock from 1798 to 1805, when he moved to Bradford. In the north he not only pastored, but also became the president of Horton Academy. See Thomas Steadman, *Memoir of the Rev. William Steadman, D.D.* (London: Thomas Ward, 1838); Sharon James, "William Steadman (1764–1837)," in *The British Particular Baptists, 1638–1910*, ed. Michael A. G. Haykin (Springfield, MO: Particular Baptist, 2000), 2:162–81.

48. As Fuller wrote to Carey on April 18, 1799: "I sometimes say Woe is me, for I am born to be a man of strife! Here are Arminians, Socinians, & final Restitutionists always provoking me to write. I seem like a sort of pugilist, who having made a little noise in the world draws upon himself every one that fancies he can master him." See "The Letters of Andrew Fuller—Copied from Various Sources," typescript ms., transcribed by Joyce A. Booth and collected by Ernest A. Payne (Angus Library, Regent's Park College, University of Oxford).

has been related. Then, in the early 1790s, it was the growing threat of anti-Trinitarian Socinianism, the leading heterodox movement of the late eighteenth century, that dominated Fuller's thinking as he wrote an extensive work against its principal apostle, namely, Joseph Priestley (1733–1804).[49] In this letter to Steevens, Fuller now refers to both of these theological conflicts:

> I feel a sacred satisfaction in the principles I have endeavoured to state and define. They are such in the main that I can venture upon for eternity. Those which I have attempted to refute still appear to me, and that with abundantly increasing evidence, to be the bane of the churches. They unnerve the Christian for spiritual activity. By what I have read and written in the Socinian controversy, I feel more attached to the great doctrines of Christ's deity and atonement, together with those of salvation by grace alone, from first to last. These truths are not merely the objects of my faith, but the ground of all my hope, and administer what is superior to my daily bread. Excuse this egotism.[50]

From Fuller's perspective, the principles of high Calvinism undermined the spirituality of Christian congregations, for they discouraged mission and evangelism and provided ground for antinomianism. Refuting Socinianism, on the other hand, had deepened Fuller's commitment to Christ's deity and his substitutionary atonement, as well as the Reformation assertion that salvation is "by grace alone, from first to last."[51]

---

49. For this work, see Andrew Fuller, *The Calvinistic and Socinian Systems Examined and Compared, as to their Moral Tendency*, in *Complete Works of the Rev. Andrew Fuller*, 2:108–233. Edward Hitchin (d. 1774), minister of White's Row Independent Chapel, Spitalifields, wrote to Priestley's cousin, also named Joseph Priestley, in 1768 that the famous author's "pride is likely to burst him—He is the Solomon of our Infidels." See *Samuel Gedge Catalogue XXIII* (Norwich, UK: Samuel Gedge, n.d.), 63.

50. Fuller, Letter to Steevens, May 18, 1793, 455.

51. Fuller later told Steevens that he hoped his work against Priestley would "demolish the Socinian scheme" (Letter to Steevens, April 14, 1795, 495). For another reference to Socinianism in these letters to Steevens, see Andrew Fuller, Letter to Thomas Steevens, June 19, 1795, in "Extracts from the Late Rev. A. Fuller's Correspondence," 496.

In addition to these remarks about the missionary society and his writing projects, Fuller also comments on Steevens's letters: "Art thou nervous, brother? Thy letters include so much sweet and savory pleasantry, that they are almost enough to cure a man that is so. I had almost said, 'Physician, heal thyself' [Luke 4:23]."[52] Since none of Steevens's letters to Fuller are extant, it cannot be known what exactly drew forth this praise of Steevens's prose as giving Fuller "sweet and savory" enjoyment. Fuller's concluding remarks once again mention Zenas Trivett and his desire for fellowship with him and Steevens: "Remember me affectionately to Mr. Trivet, when you see him, our hearty thanks await him for his exertions. If I should come a little before harvest, we must all three be together as much as possible."

"THINKING OF THOSE WHOM I LOVE"

Fuller was able to visit Steevens in Colchester and Trivett at Langham that September, a visit that he told Steevens on October 5 that he would "always remember ... with pleasure." Fuller goes on to comment about his desire to be closer geographically to Steevens: "I wish I could oftener enjoy your company, but Providence has ordered it otherwise, and, no doubt, wisely ordered it. If we do good, as salt in the earth, it must be by being spread."[53] Fuller had obviously found in Steevens a kindred spirit, but Fuller's evangelical passion to be "doing good" led him to recognize the wisdom of God's providential ordering of their lives.[54]

Fuller then mentions a meeting of the pastors of the Northamptonshire Association, which happened on a regular basis and was crucial in the formation of Fuller's appreciation of the necessity of spiritual conversation and friendship. It had been "pleasant and profitable," especially since Samuel Pearce and Benjamin Francis (1735–99) of Horsley, Gloucestershire, had been present and preached. "They are excellent men of God," Fuller

---

52. Fuller, Letter to Steevens, May 18, 1793, 455.

53. Fuller, Letter to Steevens, October 5, 1793, 494.

54. In a diary entry for July 18, 1794, Fuller comments about Acts 10:38: "It seemed a lovely thing which is said of Christ, 'He went about doing good'!" (McMullen and Whelan, *Diary of Andrew Fuller*, 188).

comments.[55] After a couple of remarks on the state of his physical health, Fuller comments on his struggle with depression, and here also Fuller found a kinship with Steevens: "I suppose I am little akin to you, though cheerful in company, frequently dejected alone; with this difference, that mine is not the hypochondriac affection (so, I think, your complaints are called,) but a kind of constitutional gloom."[56] In his recent biographical study of Fuller, Peter J. Morden has persuasively shown that from 1782 to 1792 Fuller wrestled with both spiritual and clinical depression. His involvement in the founding of the Baptist Missionary Society eventually enabled him to emerge from this spiritual winter, when he was, to employ a title from Puritan Thomas Goodwin (1600–1679), "a child of light walking in darkness."[57] As this letter to Steevens reveals, however, he was still wrestling with depression a year after the founding of the Baptist Missionary Society.

Certainly not helping this struggle with depression was a hymn written by John Fawcett that Fuller sang or read during this period. As he told Steevens:

> I never had any talent for composing hymns, yet I read the hymns of others with much pleasure. How often have I, of late, wept, in reading, or singing over the 324th hymn of Rippon's Selection, written by my dear friend Fawcett.—Also the 254th of the same selection, and composed by the same hand. Do read and sing it over, and think of me, and others. I have been ready to shed tears of joy while I have been singing it, in thinking of those whom I love, not only at and about Kettering, but in Yorkshire, in Birmingham, in Bristol,

---

55. Fuller, Letter to Steevens, October 5, 1793, 494. For Francis, see Thomas Flint, "A Brief Narrative of the Life and Death of the Rev. Benjamin Francis, A.M.," annexed to John Ryland Jr., *The Presence of Christ the Source of eternal Bliss. A Funeral Discourse, … occasioned by the Death of the Rev. Benjamin Francis, A. M.* (Bristol, 1800), 33–76; Geoffrey F. Nuttall, "Questions and Answers: An Eighteenth-Century Correspondence," *BQ* 27 (1977–78): 83–90; Michael A. G. Haykin, "Benjamin Francis (1734–1799)," in Haykin, *British Particular Baptists*, 2:16–29.

56. Fuller, Letter to Steevens, October 5, 1793, 494.

57. Peter J. Morden, *The Life and Thought of Andrew Fuller (1754–1815)*, Studies in Evangelical History and Thought (Milton Keynes, UK: Paternoster, 2015), 103–9.

in Hampshire, in Cambridgeshire, in London, in Essex, and
(I hope by this time, nearly) in Indostan!

You have indulged yourself in many a solitary hour in
composing hymns.—You have volumes of them.—Probably
some of the notes of your plaintive soul might sound in
unison with my feelings.—Would it be too much to ask you
to send me a volume of them, by Mr. Perkins? I will peruse
them about a year, and then return them.[58]

"Rippon's Selection" was, of course, John Rippon's (1751–1836) justly
popular *A Selection of Hymns, From the Best Authors*, which was first published
by this Baptist author in 1787 and over the course of Rippon's lifetime went
through thirty-one editions.[59] Fuller's citation of it here illustrates the way it
became de facto "*the* Baptist collection" of hymns for Baptist congregations
in the British Isles and America.[60]

By 1793 four editions of the hymnal had appeared, and all four listed
John Fawcett's "Thus Far My God Hath Led Me On" as hymn number 324.
Its first three stanzas are not at all uplifting, but, as Fuller had experienced,
they are all too frequently true in the lives of God's saints:

> Thus far my God hath led me on,
> And made his Truth and Mercy known;
> My Hopes and Fears alternate rise,
> And Comforts mingle with my Sighs.
> Thro' this wide Wilderness I roam,
> Far distant from my blissful Home;
> Lord, let thy Presence be my Stay,
> And guard me in this dangerous Way.
> Temptations every where annoy,
> And Sins and Snares my Peace destroy;

---

58. Fuller, Letter to Steevens, October 5, 1793, 494–95.

59. Ken R. Manley, *"Redeeming Love Proclaim": John Rippon and the Baptists*, Studies in Baptist History and Thought 12 (Carlisle, UK: Paternoster, 2004), 82–138, 295–97.

60. Manley, *"Redeeming Love Proclaim,"* 136.

My earthly Joys are from me torn,
And oft an absent God I mourn.

The other hymn, numbered 254 by Rippon, is Fawcett's most well-known hymnic piece, "Blest Be the Tie That Binds."[61] Given its theme of the blessing of Christian friendship in both this world and eternity, it is not surprising that as Fuller sang or read it he was moved to "shed tears of joy." The following stanzas brought joy and love flooding into his heart as he thought of Christian friends in the north of England, its west country, its capital, and East Anglia:

> Blest be the tie that binds
> Our hearts in Christian love;
> The fellowship of kindred minds
> Is like to that above.
> Before our Father's throne
> We pour our ardent pray'rs;
> Our fears, our hopes, our aims are one,
> Our comforts and our cares.
> We share our mutual woes;
> Our mutual burdens bear;
> And often for each other flows
> The sympathizing tear.[62]

Fuller, like Fawcett, believed such fellowship to be a rich foretaste of the future when "perfect love and friendship [will] reign/Thro' all eternity."[63]

As Fuller observed, Steevens himself was also a hymnwriter. According to his memoir in *The Baptist Magazine*, he composed "nearly two thousand

---

61. For a discussion of the context and theology of this hymn, see Haykin, *"Blest Be the Tie,"* 23–29.

62. John Rippon, *A Selection of Hymns, From the Best Authors*, 4th ed. (London, 1792), hymn #254, stanzas 1–3. Fawcett had titled this hymn "Brotherly Love" (Haykin, *"Blest Be the Tie,"* 26). Rippon changed the title to "Love to the Brethren."

63. Rippon, *Selection of Hymns*, hymn #254, stanza 6.

hymns." In the words of the unknown author of this memoir, Steevens "took considerable pleasure in versifying."[64] Now, he must have shown Fuller some of the volumes of his handwritten hymns when they met—hence Fuller's request to borrow some of them. His reason for doing so is noteworthy: "Probably some of the notes of your plaintive soul might sound in unison with my feelings." Fuller's perusal of Steevens's hymns would, in his mind, be a further means of cementing their friendship. This section of Fuller's letter on hymns especially bears out Morden's observation regarding the Baptist theologian that he was "a deep thinker who also felt with a real intensity. ... Behind the phlegmatic exterior was a man of tender conscience and strong emotions."[65]

There are three further letters, from 1795 to 1797, in this slice of correspondence between these two eighteenth-century pastors. In these letters Fuller makes further reference to his work against Socinianism, as well as his plans to write something on deism, his ongoing problems with high Calvinism, and the mission to India, in all of which Steevens would have been vitally interested in.[66] Regretfully, there do not appear to be any further extant letters of Fuller to Steevens or vice versa. But what these eight letters do powerfully reveal is the way that Fuller used the medium of the letter to engage in "free and friendly communication of [his] thoughts" to his fellow pastor Steevens and in this way make their friendship a means of grace for both of them.

---

64. "Memoir of the Rev. Thomas Steevens," 87. Some of them were later published in James Upton, *A Collection of Hymns*, 2nd ed. (London, 1815), hymns #322–48. This hymnal went through three editions by 1818. For help with obtaining this hymnal I am indebted to Chris Fenner, music and media archivist, The Southern Baptist Theological Seminary, and Kathryn Sullivan of the Bowld Music Library, Southwestern Baptist Theological Seminary.

65. Morden, *Life and Thought of Andrew Fuller*, 108. See also Charles Bumgardner, "'A Musical Pronunciation of Affecting Truth': The Church Music of Andrew Fuller" (unpublished paper, 2013), 12–16, on the impact of hymnody on Fuller's personal life.

66. Fuller, Letter to Steevens, April 14, 1795; Andrew Fuller, Letter to Thomas Steevens, June 19, 1795, in "Extracts from the Late Rev. A. Fuller's Correspondence," 495–96; Andrew Fuller, Letter to Thomas Steevens, February 7, 1797, in "Extracts from the Late Rev. A. Fuller's Correspondence," 496.

"AN OLD ENEMY OF MINE"

Charles Spurgeon's Spirituality of
the Word during His Depression

BRIAN ALBERT

In late 1890, Charles Spurgeon (1834–92) crept slowly to the pulpit. He was to deliver the sermon at the annual Mildmay Park Conference. With each ascending step, the preacher's body creaked like an unoiled door hinge. Supported by his walking stick and the countless prayers of the saints, Spurgeon did preach the message he titled "Our Leader through the Darkness." Oblivious to both speaker and audience, Spurgeon had less than two years to live. Ironically, the conference dedicated to raising funds for medical relief featured as its keynote preacher one who was in unimaginable pain with little to no reprieve. The chronic nephritis, better known as Bright's disease, had for many years slowly deteriorated his health, causing gout, sciatic, lumbago, inflammation, nerve damage, digestive problems, swelling, and headaches. Bright's disease was slowly killing the formidable pastor, and by the time his doctors diagnosed the malady, the disease was terminal. This relentless illness coupled with overwork, nervousness, stress, and public scrutiny contributed to regular depression that spanned most of his life.[1]

---

1. I address Spurgeon's physical maladies and other factors that led to his depression in my thesis. See William Brian Albert, "'When the Wind Blows Cold': The Spirituality of Suffering and Depression in the Life and Ministry of Charles Spurgeon" (PhD diss., Southern Baptist Theological Seminary, 2015).

In the sermon "Our Leader through the Darkness," Spurgeon provides his understanding of depression when he asks his listeners, "Do you know what exceeding heaviness means?" He takes his grasp of despondency one step further and links the malady with his spirituality. Spurgeon elaborates that "depression of spirit" is "deep" and "exceeding heavy" when *"accompanied with the loss of the light of God's countenance."*[2] Depression was not merely "dullness, inertia, pessimism, and deep unhappiness," as many of his Victorian counterparts believed. To be depressed, according to Spurgeon, was to feel that God's presence was removed from one's life, which led to "extreme heaviness." The significance of this definition is best framed around Spurgeon's spirituality, of which he believed the "essence … is found in Jesus." If communion with Jesus was the "nearest, dearest, closest, most intense and most enduring relationship that can be imagined,"[3] then it is not surprising that Spurgeon crafted his understanding of depression as distance to the one whom he loved dearly.

> If the Lord be once withdrawn, if the comfortable light of his presence be shadowed even for an hour, there is a torment within the breast, which I can only liken to the prelude of hell. This is the greatest of all weights that can press upon the heart. A soul conscious of desertion by God is beyond conception unendurable. When he holdeth back the face of his throne, and spreadeth his cloud upon it, who can endure the darkness?[4]

He chooses superlatives to describe this plight. "To be forsaken of God is the *worst ill* that the most melancholy saint ever dreams of."[5] His description of

2. *MTP* 59:427 (emphasis added). Spurgeon was not the only Victorian to embrace this definition. At a public meeting of London Baptists, Reverend Peto linked the two when he stated, "When there is much depression and agony of heart … a sorrow for declining grace" (*MTP* 7:228).

3. *MTP* 20:42; 29:6.

4. *MTP* 36:134.

5. *TD* 6:31 (emphasis added).

depression is deliberately connected to this "worst condition." "The worst cloud of all is deep depression of spirit. ... Sickness, poverty, slander, none of these things are comparable to depression." A few years before this statement, Spurgeon announced, "The worst of ills is a depressed spirit; at least, I scarcely know anything that can be worse than this."[6] In an effort to bring hope to his weary readers, Spurgeon admits, "Of all things in the world to be dreaded, despair is the chief. Let a man be abandoned to despair, and he is ready for all sorts of sins. When fear unnerves him action is dangerous; but when despair has loosed his joints and paralyzed his conscience, the vultures hover round him waiting for their prey."[7] In a sermon delivered in 1886, he pictured depression as "the shadow of death." Earlier in his life he said that depression was "my horror of great darkness."[8] Consistent with these claims, Spurgeon argues that "the most deplorable picture painted [in the Scriptures] is despondency."[9] "The worst cloud of all ... the worst ills ... chief ... shadow of death ... horror of great darkness ... the most deplorable picture." These were not mere pithy, little sayings doled out to be quotable; rather, they came from a lifetime of brute experience in which, from age fifteen to his death, he never was fully liberated from "Giant Despair."[10] When he expounded a text from the Psalms, Spurgeon paused in his delivery and testified, "Here is David fighting with despondency, an old enemy of mine."[11]

THE ROLE OF SCRIPTURE IN
SPIRITUALITY DURING DEPRESSION

Gardeners and chefs know that the most effective way to extract the strongest aroma from herbs is to press the plant firmly between one's fingers until the oils are released. Spurgeon knew that the most effective way to extract

---

6. *MTP* 55:401; 59:427.

7. C. H. Spurgeon, *Words of Cheer for Daily Life* (London: Passmore and Alabaster, 1895), 117.

8. *MTP* 13:138; 32:357.

9. *NPSP* 6:286.

10. John Bunyan, *The Works of John Bunyan, Vol. 3: The Pilgrim's Progress* (Carlisle, PA: The Banner of Truth Trust, 1991), 224.

11. *MTP* 17:56.

the strongest piety from believers was for the Heavenly Father to press his children with suffering, including depression, until godliness was released, providing maximum fragrance. The good Father does not allow his child to guess at coping with depression, but he provides means to develop our spirituality by "loosening our roots; cutting the strings which bind us here below; pluming our wings for the last great flight, when, leaving earth with all its ties behind us we shall enter into the realities of the bliss which remaineth for the people of God."[12] In this sense, the means of spirituality are reminders on earth of what is awaiting us in heaven.

One of the primary spiritual tools God provides his children to counter despondency and be shaped in his image is the Bible. "Fight despondency and despair with the sword of the Spirit" was a regular mantra from the London pastor.[13] "If God's Word cannot be trusted," Spurgeon once quipped, "then are our harbours turned into whirlpools and our rocks into clouds."[14] The Scriptures were "foundational ... crucial ... central ... [and] at the heart" of Spurgeon's spirituality.[15] The Bible was to Spurgeon what an engine is to a car. Scripture's power, not his personality, drove results. In 1857, he stated, "I have marked, that if ever we have a conversion at any time, in ninety-nine cases out of a hundred, the conversion is traceable to the text, or to some Scripture quoted in the sermon, than to any trite or original saying of the preacher."[16] In the last year of his life, he replayed the same refrain, "You trace your conversion, I am sure, to the Word of the Lord; for this alone is 'perfect, converting the soul.' "[17] Thus, Spurgeon's advice to preachers was to anchor their ministry on the word of God. "I am sure that no preaching

---

12. "We may grow in some things by prosperity; but true ripeness in grace can only be obtained in adversity. Our cares, our losses, our crosses, our depression of spirits, our temptations from without and from within, these are all ripening dispensations" (*NPSP* 6:457).

13. *MTP* 37:240.

14. William Williams, *Personal Reminiscences of Charles Haddon Spurgeon* (London: Religious Tract Society, 1895), 145.

15. Peter J. Morden, *Communion with Christ and His people: The Spirituality of C. H. Spurgeon* (Eugene, OR: Pickwick, 2014), 106, 110, 112, 118, 121, 135; *MTP* 39:280; Mark Hopkins, *Nonconformity's Romantic Generation* (Eugene, OR: Wipf & Stock, 2004), 153; Lewis Drummond, *Spurgeon: Prince of Preachers* (Grand Rapids: Kregel, 1992), 569.

16. *MTP* 3:57–60.

17. C. H. Spurgeon, *The Greatest Fight in the World* (New York: Funk & Wagnalls, 1891), 18.

will last so long, or build up the church so well, as the expository. ... I cannot too earnestly assure you that if your ministries are to be lastingly useful you must be expositors. ... Be masters of your Bibles."[18] The Scriptures have such extraordinary power that the reader could "let the volume fall open as if by chance and ... still discover the same singular majesty of manner."[19] This spiritual book is for spiritual people who should study it spiritually.[20]

The aim for much of Spurgeon's ministry was to grow in one's understanding of the Bible. Books such as *Morning by Morning*, *The Interpreter*, *The Cheque Book of the Bank of Faith*, and *Evening by Evening* were all aimed at the reader getting into the word of God and finding its treasures. His work *The Bible and the Newspaper* was an effort to illustrate how one could be prompted to meditate on Scripture by reading the newspaper. In 1856, he founded the Pastors' College to train ministers in the Bible. The curriculum prioritized biblical studies. A decade later, the Colportage Association was founded to distribute Bibles and other tracts to those who could not afford these materials. In 1865, Spurgeon founded a monthly magazine that he edited and largely wrote himself for the rest of his ministry, *The Sword and the Trowel*. The title was an allusion to Nehemiah 4:17–18.

Experimental spirituality is an appropriate phrase to describe Spurgeon's relationship to the Scriptures since he was convinced that Bible study was intended to transform lives. Because of this experimental nature, the Christian should engage the Bible in a personal manner. The believer should so "eat the Bible" that "at last, you come to talk in Scriptural language, and your very style is fashioned upon Scripture."[21] When Christians immerse themselves in the Bible they can experience this personal communion with the living God.

---

18. C. H. Spurgeon, *The Sword and the Trowel* (London: Passmore and Alabaster, 1865–1902), 10:221.

19. C. H. Spurgeon, *The Clue of the Maze* (London: Passmore and Alabaster, 1892), 57.

20. "We cannot appreciate the spirituality of this book, unless God's Spirit shall help us" (*MTP* 11:349). "When one studies the Bible, they ought to look for the 'spiritual meaning' of the text" (*NPSP* 6:81).

21. *C. H. Spurgeon's Autobiography: His Diary, Letters and Records* (Pasadena, TX: Pilgrim, 1992), 4:268.

When the Book has wrestled with me; the Book has smitten me; the Book has comforted me; the Book has clasped my hand; the Book has warmed my heart. The Book weeps with me, and sings with me; it whispers to me, and it preaches to me; it maps my way, and holds my goings; it was to me the Young Man's Best Companion, and it is still my Morning and Evening Chaplain. It is a live Book: all over alive; from its first chapter to its last word it is full of strange, mystic vitality, which makes it have pre-eminence over every other writing for every living child of God.[22]

While he does not disregard creeds, he affirms the most convincing evidence for reliance on Scripture is a personal experience with God.[23]

Outsiders to scripturally saturated spirituality often think of the point of the contents of the Bible for believers primarily in terms of issues of doctrine, morality, and behavior, but for insiders a main feature of the Scriptures is that they are seen as a uniquely bountiful source of comfort, consolation, encouragement, divine promises, and emotional sentiments that correspond to their own.[24]

Like many Christians suffering from depression, Spurgeon seemed to value the Bible more during his dark nights of the soul than in his bright days of prosperity. He confesses that the Bible sustained him "in the hour of bitter

---

22. *MTP* 34:112. One should not infer that Spurgeon was opposed to standard interpretative methods in Bible study. When addressing his pastoral students, he implored them, "Study your Bible in a common-sense way; read on, and get into the spirit and meaning of the verse, chapter, or book. The way some people study it reminds me of flea catching: they pick a thought up here, then over the leaves go, and they are after another there, and holding it between thumb and finger they cry, 'Here it is, I've got it. Does not this precious verse teach so and so?' and then they go deluding souls and building up false systems with that sort of thing" (Williams, *Personal Reminiscences*, 144).

23. *MTP* 35:618.

24. Timothy Larsen, *A People of One Book: The Bible and the Victorians* (Oxford: Oxford University Press, 2011), 269.

bodily pain ... in the hour of deep depression of spirit ... in the time of cruel desertion ... and in the time of slander." Though the timing and events surrounding his depression were unpredictable, one truth was constant: "I can fall back upon the eternal verities; they are the hills from which my help cometh, and they never fail me."[25]

Over and over, he turned to its pages and found "within Scripture there is a balm for every wound, a salve for every sore."[26] His wife, Susannah, made this connection between Scripture and suffering when she referred to Spurgeon's posthumous work, a commentary on the book of Matthew, as "the tired worker's final labour of love for his Lord."[27] Spurgeon's experimental spirituality was demonstrated even in despondency when he exhorted that the Bible was not "a book to be laid away in decorous and dusty disuse, nor was it a book to be read as a task, hateful but unavoidable. Rather the Bible was a book to be read, to be believed, to be obeyed, to be enjoyed, a counselor in perplexity, a solace in trial."[28]

During personal tragedies, Spurgeon turned to Scripture as his primary means of comfort. After an unfortunate yet providential mishap with Joseph Angus (1849–93), principal of Regent's Park College, that eventually led Spurgeon away from formal divinity school, the words of Jeremiah 45:5 consoled him.[29] Following the Surrey Garden Music Hall disaster, Philippians 2:8–10 was a central text in bringing him through the tragedy.[30] Throughout many of his physical maladies, the London pastor repeatedly pondered the words, "I will never leave thee, nor forsake thee."[31] During the downgrade controversy, he turned to many Scriptures, and these became his book of daily Bible promises, *The Cheque Book of the Bank of Faith*, in which he says, "During the bitterest season of trial, the writer has stayed himself

---

25. *MTP* 39:280.

26. Spurgeon, *Greatest Fight*, 15.

27. C. H. Spurgeon, *The Gospel of the Kingdom: Commentary on Matthew* (London: Passmore and Alabaster, 1893), iii.

28. H. L. Wayland, *Charles H. Spurgeon: His Faith and Works* (American Baptist Publications Society, 1892), 38.

29. Spurgeon, *Autobiography*, 1:241–42.

30. *NPSP* 2:377.

31. *MTP* 32:37–48.

upon the Lord, and trusted his sacred promises."[32] During those moments of depression, Spurgeon's consistent language for scriptural truth was simply "the promises." "At any time when a child of God is depressed, if he goes to the Word of God, he will generally get a hold of some promise."[33] He asks his weary listeners, "When you get down in spirits and depressed ... do you not turn to the promises?"[34] The promises of Scripture provide needed medicine to sick souls. They are "an ointment for every wound, a cordial for every faintness, a remedy for every disease. Blessed is he who is well skilled in heavenly pharmacy and knows how to lay hold on the healing virtues of the promises of God."[35]

One of depression's dangers is that the dark state can cloud the minds of believers to forget the promises of God and doubt the firmness of Scripture.[36] "We err when we become so depressed by our own incapacity as to conceive doubts of God's faithfulness."[37] These "marshes of fleshly doubt" are the worst medicine for the depressed soul, which will only lapse the weary into deeper waters of despondency.[38] Portraying depression as sickness, Scripture the medicine, and himself the doctor, Spurgeon prescribes the cure for depressed souls in at least three ways. The Bible provides the depressed spiritual *energy* over their despondent lethargy, pointed *empathy* during their plight, and divine *imagery* to take their weary minds away from the doldrums of earth into the bliss of heaven.

---

32. Iain Murray, *Spurgeon v. Hyper-Calvinism: The Battle for Gospel Preaching* (Edinburgh: Banner of Truth Trust, 2000), 24.

33. *MTP* 23:119.

34. *MTP* 26:251. "When any persons say to you, 'Well, if I were to meet with a desponding person, I should not know what to do,' tell them to commence quoting a promise from the Scriptures" (*MTP* 43:579).

35. *MTP* 8:97.

36. "How many a precious text have you and I read again and again without perceiving its joyful meaning, because our minds have been clouded with despondency!" (*MTP* 33:483).

37. Spurgeon, *Sword and the Trowel*, 7:69.

38. Spurgeon knew the propensity of doubting the word of God during states of depression. "I am not a little ashamed of myself that I do not live more on high, for I know when we get depressed in spirits and down cast, and doubting, we say many unbelieving and God-dishonoring words. ... We ought not to stay here in these marshes of fleshly doubts. We ought never to doubt our God" (*MTP* 9:59).

As a boa constrictor slowly decreases the energy of its victim, the depressed will decrease in motivation to escape the doldrums the longer they spend in its clutches. They may become anxious and restless and display a form of semilunacy.[39] When a person is depressed and "bent towards the ground, the main thing is to increase his stamina and put more life into him; then his spirit revives, and his body becomes erect. In reviving the life, the whole man is renewed." The Bible is the answer to this *energy*. "It is a grand thing to see a believer in the dust and yet pleading the promise, a man at the grave's mouth crying, 'quicken me' and hoping that it shall be done." While Victorian doctors primarily turned to medicine as a stimulant or sedative, Spurgeon believed that the depressed Christian could have his spirit calmed and receive peace of mind from simple faith in the word of God.[40]

"Do you not find it so," asks Spurgeon, "that, oftentimes, a text of Scripture comes to your mind just at the moment when you were about to suffer spiritual shipwreck?"[41] Doubt and trouble can never match the *empathy* of the Scriptures for the despondent. From Abraham, the friend of God, to John the Baptist, the greatest preacher who ever lived, the Bible provides illustrations of believers who struggled with doubting God (Gen 12:10–20; Matt 11:3). Questions to God on behalf of the despondent abound in the Bible. Psalms 42 and 43 contain a dozen different questions to God about the state of the depressed (Pss 42:2, 5, 9–11; 43:2, 5). When "doubting" Thomas speaks in Scripture, he asks questions during solemn occasions (John 11:16; 14:5). Jesus asks one of the most profound questions while he is dying on the cross.[42] A good portion of the Psalms was written in times of despair,

---

39. *MTP* 24:101.

40. *TD* 4:1201.

41. *MTP* 50:84.

42. While the central meaning of Matt 27:46 is not depression, there are many points one may extrapolate to prove the empathy of Jesus to the depressed. First, he asks God "Why?" which is the most difficult interrogative to ask in times of depression. ("What?" "How?" "When?" "Who?" "Where?" questions are easier answered than "Why?") Also, "Why?" questions are generally the interrogations depressed people ask God. Rather than "What is he doing to me, God?" the despondent would be more apt to ask, "Why is he doing that to me, God?" Second, Jesus ends the statement with the personal "me." Depression takes matters personally. The despondent typically does not ask, "God, why are you doing that to them?" Rather, "God, why are you doing this to me?" Third, Jesus is unafraid to address the action done against

and Jeremiah wrote an entire book about weeping. The book of Habakkuk does not end with happily ever after, martyrs in heaven are depicted as pleading for God to stop the killing, and the mothers of Bethlehem babies weep with Rachel as they recover their sons' dead bodies (Hab 3:17; Rev 6; Matt 2:16–18).[43] Part of the redemptive quality of the Lord Jesus is his assumption that people will be depressed and find their rest in him (Matt 11:28; John 4:14).[44] If depressed individuals want empathy, they will not obtain that ministry in their doubts and troubles, but they should trust the promises of the Scriptures. When this occurs, they will find there are "no handkerchiefs for the tears of saints like those which are folded up within the golden box of God's Word."[45]

Finally, Spurgeon uses remarkable *imagery* about the Scriptures to aid the depressed in overcoming their doubts and troubles. He asked the depressed to imagine encountering Jesus in the flesh. After such an experience, Spurgeon surmises, "The very spot of ground on which it occurred would be exceedingly dear and sacred to my spirit." But in times of depression, one may think it was only "a delusion, a figment of imagination, a delirium, and nothing more." Taking a cue from the apostle Peter, Spurgeon testifies that the Bible is to be trusted more than whether such an experience occurred

---

him, which is being "forsaken." While the earlier "I thirst" is a cry of need, this statement is a cry of total desperation. Given that Jesus addresses the Almighty not as his Father but as his God, and that no disciple except John is present (although Matthew's Gospel does not mention John's presence), only heightens this despair. Perhaps the absolute worst feeling of a depressed Christian is the feeling of being abandoned, deserted, and left alone by God. This is perhaps the worst description about hell, a place where God is not present in the way he is everywhere else ("depart from me"). Finally, Jesus' address to "God" coupled with "you" takes on personal responsibility. The depressed easily fall into this accusatory tone, "You are God, you are supposed to be good, and you could have prevented this!"

43. There is a reason most people do not sing the lyrics to "The Coventry Carol" during the Christmas season. The song is usually presented as an instrumental piece. The last two stanzas in particular are so depressing they are difficult to sing. "Herod the King, in his raging, Charged he hath this day; His men of might, in his own sight, All children young, to slay. Then woe is me, poor Child, for Thee, And ever mourn and say; For Thy parting, nor say nor sing, By, by, lully, lullay." See Hugh Keyte and Andrew Parrott, eds., *The New Oxford Book of Carols* (Oxford: Oxford University Press, 1998), 118.

44. Augustine's prayer applies here. "You have made us and drawn us to yourself, and our heart is unquiet until it rests in you." See Augustine, *Prayers from the Confessions*, ed. John Rotelle (Hyde Park, NY: New City Press, 2003), 15.

45. *MTP* 33:484.

(2 Pet 1:16–21). "I am as assured that this is thy Book as I am assured of my own existence; and, hence, thou hast done better for the removal of my doubts, and for the assurance of my soul's eternal salvation, by putting thy promise in thy Book, than if thou hadst thyself personally appeared to me, and spoken with thine own voice." In another sermon, Spurgeon states that Scripture "became no longer a word in a book, but the very voice of God to our soul—even that voice of the Lord, which is full of majesty."[46] In this exercise, Spurgeon encourages his weary listeners to take up their Bibles (an object they can touch), read (an object they can see), and draw comfort from the promises (a truth they can confirm from personal experience).

On the basis of these three benefits of Scripture—energy, empathy, and imagery—Spurgeon exhorts his depressed listeners to "think of the promises, and as you handle them by thought, they will exhale a sweet perfume which will delight you." Those caught in despondency should replace their fixation on troubles, which are fleeting, with the unfailing, unchanging promises of God. Depressed believers should "prostrate ... cast your feet ... remember ... rest ... and meditate on the promises," and they will be assured they will rise out of their downcast condition. Once the despondent lean on the promises, they too will testify that "the worst forms of depression are cured when Holy Scripture is believed."[47]

Spurgeon was convinced in his own experience that Scripture should be used proactively to counter depression. He held the belief later espoused by D. Martyn Lloyd-Jones (1899–1981), who wrote, "The main trouble in this whole matter of spiritual depression in a sense is this, that we allow our self to talk to us instead of talking to our self."[48] Spurgeon practiced this advice. "You see the psalmist here talks to himself. Every man is two men; we are duplicates, if not triplicates, and it is well sometimes to hold a dialogue with one's own self. 'Why art thou cast down, O my soul'?"[49] Spurgeon then

46. *MTP* 37:16–17, 44.

47. *MTP* 1:3–4; 33:484; 35:260.

48. D. Martyn Lloyd-Jones, *Spiritual Depression: Its Causes and Its Cure* (Grand Rapids: Eerdmans, 2000), 20.

49. Spurgeon does not elaborate on his "duplicate" or "triplicate" view here. We may conclude based on his full statement that he is merely suggesting we dialogue with ourselves

shared his own procedure. "I always notice that, as long as I can argue with myself about my depressions, I can get out of them; but when both the men within me go down at once, it is a downfall indeed. When there is one foot on the solid rock, the other comes up to it pretty soon."[50]

CONCLUSION

Scripture was vital in Spurgeon's spirituality during depression, and deeply personal:

> In our darkest seasons nothing has kept us from desperation but the promise of the Lord: yea, at times nothing has stood between us and self destruction save faith in the eternal word of God. When worn with pain until the brain has become dazed and the reason well nigh extinguished, a sweet text has whispered to us its heart cheering assurance, and our poor struggling mind has reposed upon the bosom of God. That which was our delight in prosperity has been our light in adversity; that which in the day kept us from presuming has in the night kept us from perishing.[51]

He loved and depended on the Scriptures, not merely for his ministry success or victory in theological strife alone, but for his own spirituality. He was not the professional who studied the Bible as an academic exercise, but one who pursued God through his word. To the "constitutionally sorrowful," Spurgeon recommends Jeremiah and Lamentations to help "express your woes and furnish you with sympathy." To the depressed who can hear "music to the tune of your own," Spurgeon points to the readings of Job.[52] And

---

in a similar way to how we write pros and cons to make a decision. We put forth an argument and counter the argument in our minds.

50. *MTP* 43:455. Spurgeon's comments are in the exposition of the psalm after the sermon manuscript. "David chides David out of the dumps; and herein he is an example for all desponding ones. To search out the cause of our sorrow is often the best surgery for grief" (*TD* 2:467).

51. *TD* 4:1475.

52. *MTP* 18:149, 21:401.

he devoted two decades compiling the largest commentary on the Psalms ever assembled. No publisher commissioned him, and he did not expect to make a profit, yet he wrote it as a man convicted and comforted by the word.[53] The title he gave to this colossal composition can best summarize Scripture's relationship to Spurgeon's spirituality in depression. The Bible is indeed, a "treasure."

H. L. Wayland (1830–1898) was present several times throughout Spurgeon's historic career at the Metropolitan Tabernacle. Wayland recorded details as he sat spellbound by the London pastor's pulpit manner, style, and content. He was also aware of Spurgeon's own struggles with depression and was impressed by Spurgeon's use of Scripture during these times of despondency. Wayland's eyewitness account provides us with much of the spirituality of the "Prince of Preachers." Even when Spurgeon read the Scriptures, "it was no longer a volume two or three thousand years old; it became a new book. Every verse was instinct with life. ... To hear him read a psalm and comment upon it was an event. He had passed through deep waters; he had borne burdens. These things help a man to see into the Psalms, make them real to him."[54]

---

53. "I cannot hope to be financially remunerated for this effort. If only the expenses are met, I will be well content" (*TD* 3:v).

54. Wayland, *Charles H. Spurgeon*, 40.

RESCUED BY THEOLOGY

Recovering a Genuinely Biblical,
Genuinely Protestant Spirituality

R. ALBERT MOHLER JR.

As a young Christian, raised in a typically evangelical, happily revivalistic, quintessentially Southern Baptist home and church, my spiritual life was a constant roller coaster. The highs were very high, but the lows were really low. I was encouraged to trust Christ and to get busy doing the things that every Christian should do: share the faith, read the Bible, pray, be fully involved in our church, and seek out explicitly Christian forms of music, entertainment, and amusement. I was told to spend time with Christian friends. I gave myself to all these things, but I never felt obedient to Christ. I was told I should feel close to Christ. I did not feel close to Christ in any enduring sense.

In the face of my frustration, I was encouraged to try harder. I did try harder. Both directly and indirectly, I was schooled in the "higher life" forms of spirituality. It seemed that there were two different categories of Christians—those who were saved, but lived unfruitful and unhappy Christian lives, and those who were saved and went on to achieve a higher-life spirituality. Trained in evangelism and handed the "Four Spiritual Laws," I learned of two different kinds of Christians—the "carnal" believer who was saved but unspiritual and the spiritual Christian who was filled with the Holy Spirit and lived a fruitful Christian life.

This two-story vision of the Christian life was so pervasive and so taken for granted that I had no idea that there could be any other understanding of how to please God. I was as involved in church life as any teenager could be. My youth minister loved Jesus, loved youth, and loved me. He was nothing but encouraging and godly in his ministry to us. He knew nothing but the same higher-life spirituality that was the basic atmosphere of evangelical Christianity in that age. My pastor preached wonderful sermons from the Bible and pointed us to Christ, but both he and guest preachers stressed the higher-life spirituality.

Nevertheless, I was entering a spiritual depression. Whatever the higher-life Christians had, I lacked. When told to try harder, I grew only more frustrated and depressed. I went to every conference, attended every revival, and genuinely tried to devote myself to Bible reading and memorization, along with prayer.

There was enough basic gospel Christianity in the air that I breathed that sinless perfectionism was ruled out as unbiblical. So was any explicitly charismatic teaching or experience. I was promised that the indwelling Christ and the power of the Holy Spirit would, if I tried hard enough, lead me into that higher spiritual plane where I longed to be.

Sometimes I thought I was there. Most of the time I was extremely aware that I was not on any higher spiritual level at all. I fell into a natural form of adolescent spiritual legalism, and yet I knew my own heart all too well. Even when I avoided sin, I could not avoid the knowledge that I wanted to sin.

Then there were the insights that came by active observation of the Christians around me. Frankly, they did not look extraordinary at all. They did not appear to be living a purely spiritual life or to be able to master sin at all. They read all the right books, went to hear all the right speakers, were obsessively active in the church, and advocated a frenetic program of personal devotions and spiritual practices. But they did not appear to be particularly happy. Their lives seemed to be marked by the problems every other Christian faced. They could not stay in the higher life even if they thought they had achieved the higher life. I knew their kids. They were just like other kids raised in Christian families. We regularly rededicated

our lives to Christ and at times thought we had achieved that higher life. It
never lasted, and we knew it.

I began to hate myself for my inability to feel what I was supposed to
feel, pray as I was supposed to pray, and direct my heart only to things from
above. Even my Bible reading was frustrating. I believed every word I read
and every verse I memorized, but I did not feel particularly spiritual after
my reading of the Bible. Oddly, after reading the Bible at night I often felt
hungry—for a snack. I hated myself for that, too. I am supposed to hunger
for the word, but my teenage self was hungry for a cookie. I wondered, Was
I really even saved?[1]

These years marked a theological and apologetic crisis for me. In high
school I was confronted with atheist teachers and their arguments. I had
huge theological questions and needed answers. But I later realized that my
theological and apologetic crisis was really a crisis of spirituality as well. It
could not have been otherwise.

Recovery came slowly, but it came. Help came into my life through
thoughtful and faithful Christian teachers who introduced me to the entire
world of biblical theology, expository preaching, apologetics, and Christian
devotion. In short, I was introduced to historic Protestantism. Grasping for
help, I found that help in the long line of faithful Christianity that runs
from Christ and the apostles through century after century. It was that line
of truth and faithfulness that was recovered and defended in the Protestant
Reformation. It was the vision of Christianity that is truly evangelical—more
evangelical, indeed, than what I knew as evangelicalism.

The younger gospel-minded Christians of the English-speaking world
in the twenty-first century may be forgiven for not realizing that they have
been the beneficiaries of books and authors and resources that did not
exist when I was a teenager. In some cases, they did not exist (or were not
available) for far longer.

---

1. For a helpful summary of the issues involved in the higher-life spirituality see Andrew
David Naselli, *No Quick Fix: Where Higher Life Theology Came From, What It Is, and Why It's Harmful*
(Bellingham, WA: Lexham Press, 2017).

In this chapter I want to point to three major authors and teachers used by God to recover biblical spirituality in our times. I will present them as three movements in a modern reformation.

MOVEMENT ONE: J. I. PACKER AND *KNOWING GOD*

James Innell Packer was not in my screen as a teenager until as a young college student I came across his book *Knowing God* in 1978. First released in 1973, the book was not even written as a book, but as a series of articles on God written for an evangelical magazine. I bought the book because of its title, but I assumed that the title was indicating yet another book of conventional evangelical higher-life spirituality. I was wrong.

In the first place, Packer's language is different from what I was accustomed to reading. From the start, he writes in terms that are clearly theological. The conviction behind the book, he states from the start, "is that ignorance of God—ignorance of both his ways and the practice of communion with him—lies at the root of much of the church's weakness today."[2]

Packer's boldness rings from the title throughout the book. "Our aim in studying the Godhead must be to know God himself better," Packer writes. "Our concern must be to enlarge our acquaintance, not simply with the doctrine of God's attributes, but with the living God whose attributes they are."[3]

I had never read anything like this before. Here was theology and spirituality explicitly presented together. The Christian life—the real Christian life—was knowing about the one true God and *knowing God himself.* I found myself excited as I read the book. I now know what Packer knew and made clear—he was largely channeling the Reformers and the Puritans, their theology and devotion. But I had no real access to either the Reformers or the Puritans at the time. Packer was at my gateway and dragged me to classical biblical spirituality.

In one strategic passage, Packer sets the reality squarely:

---

2. J. I. Packer, *Knowing God* (Downers Grove, IL: InterVarsity Press, 1973), 12.

3. Packer, *Knowing God*, 23.

We need to face ourselves at this point. We are, perhaps, orthodox evangelicals. We can state the gospel clearly; we can smell unsound doctrine a mile away. If asked how one may know God, we can at once produce the right formula; that we come to know God through Jesus Christ the Lord, in virtue of his cross and mediation, based on his word of promise, by the power of the Holy Spirit, via a personal exercise of faith. Yet the gaiety, goodness, and unreservedness of spirit which are the marks of those who have known God are rare among us—rarer, perhaps, that they are in some other Christian circles where, by comparison, evangelical truth is less clearly and fully known.[4]

What I discovered in *Knowing God* was biblical theology with confidence and grace. Packer's argument is deeply and explicitly drawn from the Bible, and he documents his argument with scriptural citations. When I looked them up, they became only clearer. Packer clearly knew God, trusted the Bible, pointed constantly to Christ, and presented the great truths about God and the gospel with unmistakable joy. I felt that same joy in my heart. My mind and my heart were jointly moved by every page of the book, by every truth so joyously presented.

Over time, other Christians introduced me to more of Packer's writings, including articles and essays in such periodicals as *Banner of Truth*. I devoured them. It is to J. I. Packer that I owe my real introduction to the Puritans. In his book of essays *A Quest for Godliness: The Puritan Vision of the Christian Life*, Packer offers what remains the best introduction to the Puritans and authentic spirituality. Packer knew that the Puritans' orthodoxy was not a mere "theoretical orthodoxy." In his words:

They sought to "reduce to practice" (their phrase) all that God taught them. They yoked their consciences to his word, disciplining themselves to bring all activities under

---

4. Packer, *Knowing God*, 25–26.

the scrutiny of Scripture, and to demand a theological, as distinct from merely pragmatic, justification for everything that they did. They applied their understanding of the mind of God to every branch of life, seeing the church, the family, the state, the arts and sciences, the world of commerce and industry, no less than the devotions of the individual, as so many spheres in which God must be served and honoured.[5]

This idea of a practical orthodoxy, Christianity "reduced to practice," was transformative for me. It shifted the foundation and focus of the Christian life away from myself and to Christ and the triune God. The objective truth of the Christian faith, anchored without apology in Holy Scripture, is translated into practical orthodoxy. Prayer and the reading of the Bible, along with the other acts of Christian devotion, are not stepping stones to a higher life but ways to know God and to love him.

At the same period of my life as a college student, other very important truths came to me. I came to realize that the higher-life spirituality and the carnal Christian shared one thing in common—they were not found in the Bible. Though I did not yet have an adequate theological vocabulary or structure to guide me, I came to depend on the "ordinary means of grace," the reading, teaching, and preaching of God's word; the gathering of the church for worship and service; the ordinances of baptism and the Lord's Supper; and the practices commanded by Christ. Perhaps more importantly, the great shift to understanding the objective truth of the Christian faith meant trusting Christ for everything—not looking for some experiential or emotional or ecstatic experience.

I came to know Richard Baxter and John Owen and Richard Sibbes as well as John Calvin and Martin Luther and so many others. As Packer explains, "The Reformers left the church magisterial expositions of what our gracious God does for us; the Puritan legacy is equally authoritative

---

5. J. I. Packer, *A Quest for Godliness: The Puritan Vision of the Christian Life* (Wheaton, IL: Crossway, 1990), 29.

declarations of what God does in us."[6] These influences, countless to me now, came over many years with cumulative effect. I can no longer remember how I first encountered many authors or first began to piece some individual truths together. I do know that reading *Knowing God* was a transformative experience. I do know that reading Packer's works on the Puritans introduced me to a new world that helped rescue me from becoming yet another of what Packer calls "the disaffected casualties of modern evangelical goofiness."[7]

MOVEMENT TWO: JOHN PIPER AND *DESIRING GOD*

As a seminary student, and to an even greater degree as a doctoral student, I had come to identify myself with the Reformers of the sixteenth century and, through the Puritans and others, with a long line of faithful, orthodox Christianity throughout the ages. I counted Jonathan Edwards as one of my heroes, and I had the Banner of Truth volumes by Edwards in my library. Nevertheless, Edwards seemed a very remote figure to me. I honestly do not remember when I first heard of John Piper, but the reference was to his book *Desiring God*. First published in 1986, *Desiring God* had become a modern evangelical classic, defining its generation of gospel-committed young evangelicals as *Knowing God* did for the generation one step older.

Piper, a New Testament scholar who was by then pastor of Bethlehem Baptist Church in Minneapolis, shocked me (and legions of other evangelicals) by opening his book with a disconcerting self-identification. Piper called himself a "Christian hedonist."

To the evangelical mind—as Packer says, "able to smell unsound doctrine a mile away"—this confession seemed very smelly indeed. The phrase "Christian hedonist" looked and sounded like an oxymoron. Hedonism represents everything Christianity rejects. The hedonism of which I knew, whether of antiquity or more recent vintage, was all about the fulfillment of sinful passions. The epitome of hedonism was, to most American Christians, someone like Hugh Hefner, not a Baptist preacher in Minneapolis.

---

6. Packer, *Quest for Godliness*, 77.
7. Packer, *Quest for Godliness*, 33.

But then Piper stacks the deck by opening his book with reference to the first affirmation of the Westminster Shorter Catechism: "The chief end of man is to glorify God and enjoy him forever." Piper then moves to argue that his purpose is to change the "and" to "by" so that we will be persuaded that "the chief end of man is to glorify God *by* enjoying him forever."[8]

Piper is careful to define terms with specificity. He disavows any intention to commit theological innovation. He grounds Christian hedonism in God's own purpose to glorify himself. "If God were not infinitely devoted to the preservation, display, and enjoyment of his own glory, we could have no hope of finding happiness in him," Piper explains. "But if he does in fact employ all his sovereign power and infinite wisdom to maximize the enjoyment of his own glory, then we have a foundation on which to stand and rejoice."[9]

I expected to be unconvinced by Piper's argument. I did not like his use of the word "hedonist." I still do not use it to describe my own understanding of the Christian life. The word is ruined for me by the hedonism of the late twentieth century. At the same time, I want to affirm everything that Piper affirms. I also want to register my own debt to Piper for the richness of his passion for God's glory and the practicality of Christian hedonism for the faithful Christian life. The main insight I have gained from John Piper is the Christian's joyful passion for God, and God's infinitely powerful passion for sinners.

Of course, John Piper would reverse that order, and *Desiring God*, like *Knowing God*, is a brilliant affirmation of the gospel as affirmed through confessional Protestantism. In essence, Piper affirms and beautifully describes the biblical doctrine of justification by faith alone even as he offers a biblical vision of sanctification. Conversion is the "creation of a Christian hedonist." Succinctly, Piper explains: "Conversion is what happens to the heart when Christ becomes for us a Treasure Chest of holy joy. Saving faith is the heartfelt conviction that Christ is both solidly reliable and supremely

---

8. John Piper, *Desiring God: Meditations of a Christian Hedonist* (Sisters, OR: Multnomah Books, 1986, 1996), 15.

9. Piper, *Desiring God*, 33.

desirable. The newness of a Christian convert is a new spiritual taste for the glory of God."[10]

The key to understanding Piper's Christian hedonism is his insistence on using the language of passion, emotion, desire, and affection in a God-honoring way. His achievement is in doing so with such biblical precision and theological clarity. His categories have been so misused by both secular hedonism and evangelical emotionalism that they are nearly ruined for so many gospel-minded Christians. Piper's concern is that without these categories Christians are left with a deflated gospel and a truncated theology that fails to account for God's own desire and passion for his own glory—the very desire and passion that explains God's saving acts in Christ.

Reading *Desiring God* for the first time, now more than thirty years ago, I realized something quite surprising. Piper was not merely concerned that a lack of appreciation and celebration for God's passion and desire for his own glory—and for sinners through Christ—and the Christian's passion and desire for God's glory would lead to a distorted Christian life. His concern was that such lack of appreciation and celebration would lead to a distortion of the gospel itself. "The pursuit of joy in God is not optional. It is not a 'extra' that a person might grow into after he comes to faith. Until your heart has hit upon this pursuit, your 'faith' cannot please God. It is not saving faith."[11]

This brings us back to Edwards, whose towering work Piper introduces as "inescapably biblical."[12] As Piper cites Edwards in defending the Great Awakening, even as it was under criticism for emotional excesses: "I should think of myself in the way of my duty, to raise the affections of my hearers as high as I possibly can, provided they are affected with nothing but truth and with affections that are not disagreeable to the nature of what they are affected with."[13]

---

10. Piper, *Desiring God*, 66.

11. Piper, *Desiring God*, 69.

12. Piper, *Desiring God*, 90.

13. Jonathan Edwards, *Treatise Concerning the Religious Affections* (Edinburgh: Banner of Truth Trust, 1974), cited in Piper, *Desiring God*, 91.

Edwards goes on to warn: "The things of religion are so great, that there can be no suitableness in the exercises of our hearts, to their nature and importance, unless they be lively and powerful. In nothing is vigor in the actings of our inclinations so requisite, as in religion; and in nothing is lukewarmness so odious."[14]

The great liberation for me in reading the Puritans and Edwards, and later reading Piper, was in realizing that there was indeed an authentically emotional dimension of the Christian life as defined by Scripture and expressed supremely in the gospel of Jesus Christ. There is a role for the affections, exulting in the joy of knowing God through Christ. There is a rightful and healthy and essential role for passion in the Christian life and the Christian ministry.

And Piper affirmed, defended, and exalted doctrine, right doctrine, doctrine as revealed in God's word. He affirmed the great doctrines of the Reformation passionately. And he defended and celebrated the full truthfulness and authority of God's word. Furthermore, Piper in his books and in his ministry reveals a glad dependence on the ordinary means of grace.

MOVEMENT THREE:
DONALD WHITNEY AND OBEYING GOD

If "hedonism" had been ruined for me, the same was almost true for the term "spirituality." During my college and seminary days, "spirituality" in the larger culture merely referred to a vague, nondescript, nonbiblical notion that generally implied a form of mysticism. I knew what Roman Catholics meant by spirituality, having read figures such as Thomas Merton and Thomas à Kempis. I knew what Protestant liberals meant by spirituality, having been exposed quite thoroughly to modern mystics in the course of my studies. I yearned for a biblical spirituality, but almost everyone who used the word betrayed a theological structure that I could not follow.

---

14. Jonathan Edwards, "The True Excellency of a Gospel Minister," in *The Works of Jonathan Edwards* (Carlisle, PA: Banner of Truth Trust, 1959), 2:958, cited in Piper, *Desiring God*, 91.

Figures such as Richard Foster and Dallas Willard were appreciated by many evangelicals, but both were too mystical to help me. Having been rescued from confusion by Reformed theology and wanting to follow a path obedient to Scripture, I was reluctant to identify with any use of the word "spirituality."

Yet ... the word is biblical. The Bible speaks of "you who are spiritual" (Gal 6:1) assisting those who are less mature. There must be some rightful use of the term, some healthy and faithful exercise of what would rightly be called a biblical spirituality.

In the current generation, no single figure has contributed more than Donald S. Whitney to the definition and the defense of biblical spirituality. His most important book, *Spiritual Disciplines of the Christian Life* (first published in 1991 and updated in a new edition in 2014), is a singular contribution to the recovery of a genuinely biblical and evangelical spirituality—a spirituality consonant with Scripture, consistent with the gospel, and recognizable to the Reformers, the Puritans, and their heirs.[15]

As Whitney explains: "The Spiritual Disciplines are those practices found in Scripture that promote spiritual growth among believers in the Gospel of Jesus Christ. They are the habits of devotion and experiential Christianity that have been practiced by the people of God since biblical times."[16]

In other words, they represent the practices found in Scripture that define obedience to Christ and spiritual health. Whitney insists on biblical authority for such practices and disciplines, assured that they are "derived from the gospel, not divorced from the gospel," and made clear that are to be seen as means and not as ends. The end, he affirms, is godliness. The disciplines are the means used by the Holy Spirit in conforming believers to godliness.

Once again, we see an unambiguous affirmation of the ordinary means of grace. Once again, we see Scripture underlined as the infallible and inerrant revelation of God. Once again, we see a gospel-centric form of

---

15. Donald S. Whitney, *Spiritual Disciplines of the Christian Life* (Colorado Springs: NavPress, 1991; rev. ed., 2014).

16. Whitney, *Spiritual Disciplines*, 4.

Christian devotion that is consistent with the doctrines of the Bible and the authentic evangelical heritage.

We also see a pattern of biblical practices defined in terms of disciplines— perhaps best understood as the practices that Christ commanded to his disciples. A genuine biblical spirituality is nothing more than obedience to Christ and doing what the Scripture reveals we ought to do—in other words, the spiritual disciplines of the Christian life.

Whitney begins with the Bible, and he turns to commend both Scripture memorization and the practice of meditation. Memorization is commanded in Scripture, but so is meditation on God's word. Whitney understands the problem:

> One sad feature of our contemporary culture is that meditation has become identified more with non-Christian systems of thought than with biblical Christianity. Even among believers, the practice of meditation is often more closely associated with yoga, transcendental meditation, relaxation therapy, or some New age practice than with Christian spirituality. Because meditation is so prominent in many spiritually counterfeit groups and movements, some Christians are uncomfortable with the whole subject and suspicious of those who engage in it.[17]

But Whitney comes back to define a biblical understanding of Christian meditation by arguing, "Let's define meditation as deep thinking on the truths and spiritual realities revealed in Scripture, or upon life from a spiritual perspective, for the purposes of understanding, application, and prayer."[18]

We could hardly imagine a more biblical notion than that. Later, Whitney defines meditation as "the missing link between Bible intake and prayer."[19]

---

17. Whitney, *Spiritual Disciplines*, 46.
18. Whitney, *Spiritual Disciplines*, 46–47.
19. Whitney, *Spiritual Disciplines*, 86.

For me, perhaps the most helpful suggestion of a specific spiritual discipline is Whitney's notion of "praying the Bible." As he explains, the human mind is so finite, so distracted, and so transient that all Christians have difficulty in prayer. The pattern is to find that we say and think the same things repeatedly. We lose our train of thought. We want to think about the infinite glory of the triune God, and yet we find our minds drifting. We want to think of Christ, but we end up thinking about the calendar ... or wanting a cookie.

Whitney commends praying the Bible, and the practice makes perfect sense. Consistent with his argument for meditation on Scripture, Whitney argues that we should "pray through a passage of Scripture, particularly a psalm."[20] As he later explains, praying the Scripture even awakens the Christian's heart to want to pray: "If you go to pray and your heart is cold as ice spiritually, you can take the fire of God's Word and plunge it into your frosty heart by praying through a passage of Scripture. Then very soon ... the Word of God warms your heart to the things of God, and you begin to feel like praying."[21]

Whitney has expanded his thought through a series of books, including the published version of his dissertation on Edwards, *Finding God in Solitude: The Personal Piety of Jonathan Edwards and Its Influence on His Pastoral Ministry.*[22] In this book, Whitney makes a convincing case for Edwards as a continuation of the Puritan tradition and for his personal piety as consistent with his pastoral ministry. Edwards, Whitney argues, was a man marked by an "introverted personality" and an "analytical disposition," and a man whose spiritual disciplines and concern for the religious affections were congruent with both Scripture and his own approach to pastoral work. Citing Martyn Lloyd-Jones, who identifies Edwards as "the very zenith or acme of Puritanism," Whitney concludes by declaring that "Edwards considered the practice of personal

---

20. Donald S. Whitney, *Praying the Bible* (Wheaton, IL: Crossway, 2015), 27.

21. Whitney, *Praying the Bible*, 85.

22. Donald S. Whitney, *Finding God in Solitude: The Personal Piety of Jonathan Edwards and Its Influence on His Pastoral Ministry* (New York: Peter Lang, 2014).

piety to be as necessary and desirable for the soul as the practice of eating and drinking was for the body."[23]

As I have hoped to demonstrate, all three of these authors have contributed greatly to my own understanding and practice of the Christian life. All three of the main books identified in this article, *Knowing God*, *Desiring God*, and *Spiritual Disciplines of the Christian Life*, have made a deep imprint on modern evangelicalism, and for great good.

---

23. D. Martyn Lloyd-Jones, *The Puritans: Their Origins and Successors* (Edinburgh: Banner of Truth Trust, 1987), 351, cited in Whitney, *Finding God in Solitude*, 145; Lloyd-Jones, *Puritans*, 147.

THE SPIRITUAL ADVANTAGES OF FAITH IN DIVINE PROVIDENCE

Heidelberg Catechism, Question 28

JOEL R. BEEKE

As Christians, we believe that God will provide.[1] This truth is the necessary consequence of the covenant promise, "I will be a God unto thee, and to thy seed after thee" (Gen 17:7).[2] Providence is, as Reformed theologians have always insisted on biblical grounds, God's being God, God's acting according to his own nature, God's accomplishing his eternal counsel in time and space, and God's keeping his promises to his children—that is, to all who are joined to Christ by a true faith.

There is no limit to the operations of God's providence. There is no limit on God's part, since providence is the almighty and everywhere-present power of God himself. "With God nothing shall be impossible" (Luke 1:37). Nor is there any limit on what providence can do for us, since there is no one in heaven or on earth and nothing in our experience that lie beyond the reach of God's power and steadfast love. The God who created all

---

1. I delivered an abbreviated form of this chapter as an address at the Greenville Presbyterian Theological Seminary's annual conference in March 2014.

2. Unless otherwise noted, all Scripture quotations in this chapter follow the KJV.

things upholds all that he has made and governs all his creatures and all their actions.

In this chapter, I want to move beyond discussing the definition of divine providence and its beauty in our eyes as those who believe in this God who provides. I want to carry the discussion one step further and consider the advantages of knowing and believing that God created all things, upholds all things, and governs all things.

I want to consider question 28 of the Heidelberg Catechism and answer the question, In what way, really, does the providence of God profit me personally? This is where the Heidelberg Catechism excels. It is a book of comfort, and question after question begins this way: "What advantage is this doctrine for you?" "What profit is it for you?" "What comfort is it to you?"

> Question 28: What advantage is it to us to know that God has created, and by His providence doth still uphold all things?
>
> Answer: (1) That we may be patient in adversity; (2) thankful in prosperity; and (3) that in all things, which may hereafter befall us, we place our firm trust in our faithful God and Father, that nothing shall separate us from His love (Romans 8); since all creatures are so in His hand, that without His will they cannot so much as move.

Let us first reflect on the particular form of the question before proceeding to examine the answer.

A SHOCKING QUESTION?

If you are not familiar with the Heidelberg Catechism, the way the question is put may be a bit of a shock. "What advantage is it?" The question may strike you as somewhat crass or a bit too pragmatic. Should we not value truth for its own sake? Is it right to think in terms of practical benefits or advantages that may accrue to us for believing a particular doctrine? Is utility or practical value a proper standard for determining what humanity is to believe concerning God and what duty God requires of people?

First, we must note that the doctrine has already been set forth as a biblical truth in the catechism, as something God has revealed in his word (question 20), and on very good grounds. Even if it could be shown to be of no practical value at all, this doctrine would still be true. The question of profit, advantage, or practical value is not the starting point, but only a secondary consideration.

At the same time, it is still a biblical question. Christ himself poses it: "What is a man profited, if he shall gain the whole world, and lose his own soul?" (Matt 16:26). Paul asks, "What advantage then hath the Jew? or what profit is there of circumcision?" (Rom 3:1). He warns the Galatians "that if ye be circumcised, Christ shall profit you nothing" (Gal 5:2). Concerning the generation of Israelites that perished in the wilderness, he notes that "the word preached did not profit them, not being mixed with faith in them that heard it" (Heb 4:2). James asks, "What doth it profit, my brethren, though a man say he hath faith, and have not works?" (Jas 2:14).

So, the framers of the catechism were on solid ground to raise this question once the doctrine itself had been set forth in a biblically faithful manner. In fact, questions such as this one are a feature of the section of the catechism devoted to expounding the twelve articles of the Apostles' Creed in Lord's Days 7 through 23 (questions 22–59). Clearly the catechism wants to alert us to the practical value of many of the things we hold to be true.

No less than eight times, the question is put in one way or another, What does it profit you now that you believe this? Various words are used; the question is posed in terms of advantage (questions 28, 49), benefit (43), profit (51, 59), and comfort (52, 57, 58). The three uses of the word "comfort" show plainly that what the catechism has in view is *spiritual advantage*, benefit, and profit, and not anything material. Modern evangelical preachers sometimes seem to have forgotten this distinction and have substituted a false gospel of self-esteem, material advantage, and worldly success for the historic gospel of divine grace, pardon for sins, and the gift of eternal life.

We should also note in passing that the book of Proverbs, setting forth "Laws from Heaven for Life on Earth,"[3] bears eloquent witness to the fact that the Bible sees no necessary opposition or conflict between truth and practical value. So, there is good reason for the catechism to ask, "What advantage is it to know that God has created, and by His providence doth still uphold and govern them?"

A SPIRITUAL CHALLENGE

The answer to this question is given in terms that pose a fundamental challenge to every Christian. Step by step, the truth of divine providence is applied to the heart in the midst of our present circumstances in life and in the face of an unknown future. We are challenged to throw off habits of life and thought that are considered only natural and quite forgivable (if forgiveness be needed at all!) by most human beings. We are challenged to live and walk by faith in the daily things of life and to trust in God under adverse circumstances in the presence of deadly spiritual peril and, most of all, with respect to what the future holds in store for us. There are three catechism themes that profit us when we exercise faith in God's providence; let us look at each of them in some depth.

Trusting God When Things Go Wrong

According to question 28, the first advantage of faith in the providence of God is "that we may be patient in adversity." Notice first that the catechism takes for granted that everyone must face adversity in this life. The entrance of sin into the world turned our earthly paradise into a battleground or minefield. We have made ourselves enemies to the very planet we live on. We Americans enjoy a high standard of living and can look forward to a long life. But for millions of others in the world today, life remains what it always has been for humankind in general: short, harsh, toilsome, and beset with trouble. Nevertheless, for all of us it remains true: "Man is born unto trouble, as the sparks fly upward" (Job 5:7).

---

3. William Arnot, *Studies in Proverbs: Laws from Heaven for Life on Earth* (repr., Grand Rapids: Kegel, 1978).

Our forefathers of the sixteenth and seventeenth centuries thought very differently about adversity than we do. We wish each other a happy new year, and we mean, for the most part, "I hope you don't have much adversity this year." The Puritans said to each other, "Blessed New Year," which means a truly happy new year, but by it they meant, "I hope that whatever God in his inscrutable providence deems fitting to place upon you this year will be sanctifying to your soul." That is a very different way of living.

Modern people, perhaps more than in any other age, do not respond well to adversity—especially in America, where we are so used to being pampered and we have so many material possessions. The night before I was to deliver the address that has become this chapter, I got word that my flight the next afternoon was canceled. I needed to get up to New Jersey and meet with some people that evening, and my first thought was, "You have got to be kidding!" But my second thought was, "And you are the guy who is going to preach about patience in adversity tomorrow morning?" Our natural response to adversity is negative, but our instructor speaks to us that this is the profit of really drinking in and believing that God governs all things through his will for his glory and for our good, and that we must respond with patience in adversity.

Our natural response to adversity is to resent it, to sink into self-pity, to complain of all that we must suffer at its hands, and to struggle in vain to escape or avoid it. Many of us blame God in our hearts and have a quarrel with the Almighty: "Why hast thou made me thus?" (Rom 9:20).

Such behavior, though common to humankind, is quite destructive and only increases the terrible toll that adversity exacts from us. Anger and resentment provide fertile soil for roots of bitterness that spring up to trouble us and defile many (Heb 12:15), even entire nations. The defeat Germany suffered in World War I left many Germans angry and resentful. Their anger stoked the fires of hatred for the Jews among them, who were charged with having stabbed Germany in the back. Their resentment grew against the victorious Allies. So, they willingly followed Hitler into an even more horrible war against all of Europe, resulting in an even more humiliating and destructive defeat.

Thus, people and nations react badly when the dark clouds of adversity bear down on them. The challenge for Christians facing adversity is, first, to cease from anger and die to natural feelings of resentment. They must walk by faith, which means holding fast to what they know about God's love for them in Christ, God's faithfulness in keeping his promise, and, most importantly, God's holy purposes in sending evil on them in this vale of tears.

Patience in adversity, therefore, goes far deeper than simply resigning yourself to what happens to you because you cannot change it. This is what many people think patience is: "I'm going to be patient and not complain because I cannot do anything about it anyway. My adversities are inevitable. I will just look at the sunny side of things as much as possible."

The Buddhist, the Muslim, and the unbeliever can, through human reason, reach this point at times. But true Christian patience goes much deeper. It is an active grace in at least four ways.

First, when we have patience in adversity *we become willing cross carriers.* Christian patience in adversity gives us strength not merely to drag our crosses and burdens through this life but to carry our crosses cheerfully behind Christ. What a world of difference there is between a cross dragger and a cross carrier. What about you? Are you dragging your crosses? Or are you carrying them behind the Lord Jesus Christ?

Second, when we have patience in adversity *we engage in wholehearted prayer.* We believe that God really governs all things and, therefore, because he ties his government to means (and one of the major means is prayer), we engage in wholehearted prayer to the living God of providence. Christian patience is more than silence. We can have much rebellion lying underneath our silences. Christian patience is the opposite of rebellion. It is not silent rebellion, but it is "unbosoming prayer," as our forefathers called it— trusting, surrendering prayer. So Christian patience is what teaches us to pray and to truly mean it: "Lord, teach me Thy will to do, and not to will what Thou dost not will."

Third, *Christian patience manifests godly conscientious watchfulness.* Puritan John Flavel puts it this way: "He that will watch providences will never want [lack] providences to watch."[4] Watchful Christian patience defies all enemies and presses on in the path of duty, waiting on God and looking for his promised deliverance in due time. Ultimately, such patience consists of lifting up our head by faith to look for Christ to come as judge from heaven, to cast all his and our enemies into everlasting condemnation, and to translate all his chosen ones to himself into heavenly joys and glory (Heidelberg Catechism, question 52).

Fourth, Christian patience teaches how to display scriptural awareness of reasons God afflicts believers. Many reasons could be included here, but I will give you just five:

1. *Suffering for the righteous is chastening in its purpose.* This is the point of Proverbs 3:5–12, picked up and cited in Hebrews 12:5 and following (see Ps 119:67, 71). We need chastening. Where would you and I be in our spiritual pilgrimages if God never chastened us—if he always answered our prayers right away and did whatever we wanted? We would be spoiled brats, spiritually immature, and self-centered, and we would actually be on our way to destruction. God chastens every son whom he loves and whom he receives (Heb 12:6). Through chastening God develops character building and spiritual maturation and enables us to grow in the grace and knowledge of the Lord Jesus Christ.

2. *God afflicts us to vindicate himself.* God likes to reveal his nature through his people. That is what he did with Job, and this is what he does with us at times. He brings us into affliction so that his graces can shine through our lives and so that people can see Christ in us. There are many people in the world today who never pick up a Bible to read. You, dear believer, and your life are the closest thing to a Bible they will ever read. If God shines with his grace and manifests and boasts of himself in and through your afflictions, then it is a worthy purpose to suffer—and you should count it all joy to suffer for his glory and for his name's sake.

Remember how Paul picks this idea up in Ephesians 3 when he says, "What God has in view for the church is that His multicolored wisdom

---

4. John Blanchard, comp., *The Complete Gathered Gold* (Darlington, UK: Evangelical Press, 2006), 515.

might be put on display to the principalities and powers, so that He can say, 'You can see that; that reflects the kind of God I am.' " Certainly in terms of our academic theology, and also pastorally, we must not lose sight of this as an element of divine providence. It takes place not only within the horizontal dimension of our relationships with one another and what we become in ourselves, but also within the vertical dimension of the ultimate conflict between the powers of God in his kingdom and the ultimate antithesis with the kingdom of darkness. In that connection, it is significant in Matthew 16:18 that the language Jesus uses sets the building of his church providentially within the context of a conflict with the powers of darkness.

3. *God often chastens us and teaches us patience under affliction so that we learn to live more eschatologically.* Not only chastisement and divine vindication but eschatological hope is a major reason for affliction. If God never chastens us, we put our tent stakes too deeply into this earth's soil. We forget we are renters here and that our eternal home is hereafter, and we begin to live comfortably in this world. But God loosens our tent stakes through affliction. As Thomas Watson says, "God would have us live in this world as if the world were a loose tooth in our mouth, which being easily twitched away doth not much bother us."[5] We are too much at home in this world and too little at home with our heavenly world.

This is a problem in our Reformed heritage too. I could never understand why in several hundred pages of his *Systematic Theology* Louis Berkhof has less than one page on heaven. I cannot understand why John Calvin has only a few pages on it in his *Institutes*. I cannot understand why even our Three Forms of Unity from the Dutch tradition and our three Westminster Standards from the British tradition have so little on heaven. It does not make sense. Heaven is our future home, and God weans us from this world by afflicting us so that we get weary of this world and long for the world to come. As the Puritan Richard Baxter said, "O that Christians were careful

---

5. Thomas Watson, *A Body of Divinity: Contained in Sermons upon the Westminster Assembly's Catechism* (Edinburgh: Banner of Truth Trust, 2000), 125.

to live with one Eye still on Christ Crucified, and with the other on Christ coming in Glory!"[6]

By failing to do this when we are afflicted, we are prone merely to see the world prospering and ourselves groaning, so we go through the "Asaph syndrome" of self-pity in Psalm 73. Happily, God leads us to the place Asaph came to in Psalm 73:17 where he stops complaining and then says he was envious "until I went into the sanctuary of God; then understood I [the wicked's] end." It is when we look eschatologically to the so-called four last things, as the Puritans called heaven, hell, judgment, and death, that we begin to understand that we need providential affliction to be prepared in God's providence to be with Christ in glory forever.

Do you know that when the Puritans meditated, they meditated more on the four last things than any other subjects? If you never were afflicted, you would seldom meditate on these things. By nature, we spend more time preparing for a two-week vacation than we do for eternity. God afflicts us so that we will get our priorities reorganized and restructured so we will begin to think about eternity.

4. *God afflicts us in terms of forming us as a blueprint* so that the gospel becomes imprinted in our lives in such a way that we grow in knowing experientially our union with Jesus Christ. There is suffering in the life of the righteous because of our union with Christ. Calvin rightly emphasized that God has so constituted the church that death is the way to life and the cross is the way to victory. Paul's language notes that when we suffer, we are filling up that which is behind in our experiential acquaintance of communion with Christ with respect to his sufferings. He is the substance; we are the shadow. Thus, we learn to follow behind him and grow in the communion that flows out of our union with him. So, we learn patience in adversity through scriptural awareness of why God calls us to suffering.

Christian patience does not mean that we may not pray for adversity to be averted or removed. But it does mean that when adversity comes, we have reasons for rejoicing because we know that God our Father is chastening us

---

6. Richard Baxter, "The Right Method for a Settled Peace of Conscience and Spiritual Comfort," in *The Practical Works of Richard Baxter* (London: Thomas Parkhurst, 1707), 2: 844.

as sons and daughters whom he loves and that he will use also our present afflictions to purify and draw us closer to him. Then we can believe with the poet William Cowper, "Behind a frowning providence, He hides a smiling face."[7]

Then too we count it all joy when we "fall into divers temptations" (Jas 1:2). "We glory in tribulations also: knowing that tribulation worketh patience; and patience, experience; and experience, hope" (Rom 5:3–4). We resolve to "run with patience the race that is set before us, Looking unto Jesus the author and finisher of our faith; who for the joy that was set before him endured the cross, despising the shame" (Heb 12:1–2).

Such patience is supernatural and superhuman. It must be given to us from above, worked in us by God's word and the Holy Spirit. The root of this patience is true faith, planted, watered, and growing up to maturity and bearing many fruits, patience in adversity being among the most valuable of such good fruits. We cannot endure in our strength because sooner or later adversity will conquer our will to resist it, and we will yield to the temptation to curse God and die. Only by Spirit-worked grace can we remain patient in adversity.

5. *We learn patience in adversity through becoming sincerely submissive.* Patience reveals itself by submissive faith in God's fatherly hand of providence. You never learn that in prosperity. This is a fruit of Spirit-worked application in adversity. But what does it mean to be submissive? Basically, the Reformers and the Puritans said it means four things.

First, it means to *acknowledge the Lord*, so that as soon as adversity comes you say, "It is the Lord"—like Eli when he hears that his sons are dead. There is no hope or future if it is not of the Lord. A few days after 9/11, Larry King asked John MacArthur and four other ministers on his show where God was in the tragedy that struck America. After the other four church leaders said that God has nothing to do with this tragedy, MacArthur stressed that if God had nothing to do with this tragedy then we are all serving an impotent God who cannot help us. God is in *everything*. That is what providence has been teaching us all along. When you become

---

7. William Cowper, *Olney Hymns* (London: W. Oliver, 1779), 328.

submissive before God, the first thing you realize of every affliction is that *it is the Lord*. The psalmist says in Psalm 39:9, "I was dumb, I opened not my mouth; because thou didst it."

Second, the next step—which is a bit deeper—is that you *justify the Lord*. You look at whatever the Lord is doing to you and you say, "Lord, it is right"—not only "It is Thee," but "It is right." Justifying the Lord is a step deeper because you are saying, "I deserve even worse."

I was recently in a hospital going from the first floor to the seventh, and a woman walked on the elevator with me. I asked her which floor she wanted; she said floor 7, and I thought, "Well, I've got about one minute to evangelize her here."

I commented, "Nice weather today."

She said, "Yes."

I said, "It's a good thing we are not in charge of the weather."

She said, "That's right; the good Lord is."

I thought that was great and said, "Yes, I guess we don't deserve this kind of beautiful weather."

She looked at me and said, "My mother always told me anything above the ground is a mercy of the Lord." Now she was evangelizing me! This was great! This is what good theology teaches: anything above death and hell *is* the mercy of the Lord.

We will look at afflictions this way when we see what we really deserve. It is only people who justify the Lord who are truly happy in life. The people in the world are not happy because they always think they have more coming. They are continually unhappy. But Christians are truly happy because they know they always deserve much worse. True happiness grows in the soil of a conscious sense of unworthiness. This can frustrate an unbeliever. It really frustrated me when I was a boy. Whenever I would complain, wanting self-pity from my mother, she would always say, "It could be worse." One day I said to her, "That is ridiculous, Mother. You say that all the time to me! You could say that about anything." And she said, "That's right; it could be worse." True Christian patience justifies God—always. It is *right*. "The LORD gave, and the LORD hath taken away" (Job 1:21).

Third—and this goes much deeper—true Christian patience in adversity not only says, "It is the Lord," and, "It is right," but it *approves the Lord;* it says, "It is well." It is one thing to acknowledge him, another thing to justify him, but another thing to approve of him. The believer who reaches this step of submission can say, "Lord, what Thou art doing in afflicting me is not only right, but it is also good; it is best. Thou art my all-knowing Father. Thou knowest the best way for Thy glory and for my good. Trusting Thee, I approve of all that Thou hast done and all that Thou wilt do. I amen all Thy ways with me." Here, you get to the real heart and the depth of Christian patience. The Shunamite woman said, "It is well," when her only son of promise was dead at home (2 Kgs 4:26). That is amazing submission! It does not mean she did not feel the pain. She still went to Elijah, clung to his feet, and said, "You must come with me." True submission feels real pain. Some people think that when you are submissive you do not feel any pain. Once a woman came to me whose husband had died about three years prior, and she said, "God has been with me so much in these three years that I don't even miss my husband." Something is not right about that. Submission that is pain-free is not submission. There is nothing to bow under. True submission is learning to say, "It is well," when it hurts deeply. I am learning to trust my Father, knowing that he makes no mistakes.

In such times of approving God while we are in adversity, we know that the adversity is for our own good. The Belgic Confession teaches that "devils and all our enemies" can indeed hurt Christians but not "without [God's] will and permission" (article 13). Knowing this truth helps us to endure adversity submissively. Without approving providence this would not be possible. As Johannes VanderKemp writes, "If no universal Ruler directed whatsoever comes to pass, how should good men be able to quiet and comfort themselves in all their tribulations? Would not their condition be worse than that of the wicked?"[8]

8. Johannes VanderKemp, *The Christian Entirely the Property of Christ, in Life and Death: Exhibited in Fifty-Three Sermons on the Heidelberg Catechism* (1810; repr., Grand Rapids: Reformation Heritage Books, 1997), 1:223.

Fourth, and finally, true submission—this is the deepest step of all—*clings to the Lord* in every situation. It clings to God during the greatest trials as the soul's best friend even when he seems to oppose us as if we were his worst enemy. We kiss the rod that strikes us and cling to the fatherly hand that chastens us. We rejoice in persecution for Christ's sake for we feel the Father's hand of love. Then, like Paul and Silas, we can sing in the "inner prison" of affliction, feeling the Father's hand of mercy.

One day I was sitting in a park in London, meditating on my sermon for the evening, when a young woman came into the park with a large dog. She had a hard ball in her hand that she threw at her dog, hitting the dog every time from about ten feet away. I thought, "That dog is going to attack her!" But the dog picked up the ball and brought it back to her, wagged his tail, and she did it again and again. I thought, "This dog models for me what I ought to do when God slams up against me with afflictions. I ought to bring the affliction back to him and just cling to him."

Job models this when he confesses, "Though he slay me, yet will I trust in him" (Job 13:15). This is what true patience in adversity ultimately means. It does not just mean you pray that all adversity will be averted. It does not mean you pray for more adversity either. William Plumer (1759–1850) devotes a chapter in his treatise on providence to "that great man of Uz." He beautifully depicts Job's patience in adversity:

> Under this enormous load of suffering Job set a bright example of patience. Not a word of sinful murmur escaped his lips (1:22). He exhibited not the proud severity of the stoic in refusing to acknowledge himself afflicted. He had not the iron hardness of atheism, denying God's hand in his troubles. Nor did he exhibit the sinful stinking of unbelief. He submissively acquiesced in what God ordained. He brought no foolish charge against his maker. He meekly says: "What!

> Shall we receive good at the hand of God, and shall we not
> receive evil?" (2:10).[9]

This kind of patience is supernatural and superhuman. We do not have it by ourselves; it must be given to us from above. We need to ask for it, and God will give it. We need to be so saturated with the proper understanding of God's fatherly providence to believers that this becomes, by the grace of the Holy Spirit, almost second nature to us. Patience in adversity is a tremendous benefit that we get from the doctrine of providence.

When my flight was canceled, I had to take the theology of providence and say, "God, there must be a good reason that I won't be making my important appointments this evening in New Jersey because my plane is canceled. Will God allow me to sit beside someone on a later plane to evangelize him or her? That might well be worth more than a thousand visits." You just do not know. God orchestrates every detail, so you just rest and say, "This is God's way." It saves all that fretting and worrying. You simply trust in the Lord and become patient in adversity.

All this is denoted by the word "patience," which means endurance under the cross of suffering. We must be patient under adversity. This does not mean that we must put up with it, to the best of our ability, in the hope that it will soon pass away. Rather, we deny ourselves, that is, we turn away from our natural feelings and desires, and we take up the cross before us as our cross and shoulder it with thankfulness.

Such patience is active, not passive. Such patience defies all enemies and presses on in the path of duty, waiting on God and looking for his promised deliverance in due time. Ultimately, such patience consists of lifting the head by faith to look for Christ to come as judge from heaven to cast all his and our enemies into everlasting condemnation and to translate all his chosen ones to himself, into heavenly joys and glory (question 52).

---

9. William S. Plumer, *Jehovah-jireh: A Treatise on Providence* (repr., Harrisonburg, VA: Sprinkle, 1997), 178.

Thanking God When Things Go Right

Even the most serious-minded Calvinist among us must admit that, in the kindness of God, things do not always go wrong in this world. God's hand is a restraining power in the world so that people cannot do all the evil they would do. Moreover, by the same hand, God continues to give good gifts to all humankind and to do good to all, the just and the unjust alike. Astonishingly, God continues to love the world, so much that he has provided a way of redemption, deliverance, and restoration through faith in Christ.

But in prosperity, that is, when things go right for us, there is a great spiritual danger. The natural tendency of fallen humanity in prosperity is to forget God and to be impressed with themselves and their ability to manage things well. People imagine that they have succeeded in life by their own efforts. Just as crosses become blessings to those who trust in God, so prosperity becomes a snare to those who are so foolish as to forget God.

It is good for us to pray for those who are suffering adversity in this life, whether it be poverty, sickness, or persecution. But it is also necessary to pray for our loved ones when they are blessed with success or prosperity in the things that pertain to this life. Adversity is a bitter cup to drink from; prosperity, like wine, has a rich red color and pleasant smell, and it sparkles in the cup. It can bedazzle and befuddle us until at last we worship our own success and God is not in all our thoughts. Even ministers of the gospel have been known to boast of their success in drawing crowds, courting the praise of people, and reveling in the perks of living in grand houses, traveling the world, and indulging in expensive recreations.

By faith, however, Christians understand that they have nothing that they have not received from the hand of God. They love the Giver far more than the gifts. As the heirs of salvation, believers know that they have already received from God far more than they could ever repay in a thousand lifetimes. The new mercies received every day only move them to thank God more and to call on their fellow human beings to praise the Lord. They delight to sing, "O give thanks unto the LORD; for He is good: because his mercy endureth forever" (Ps 118:1, 29).

I once told my theological students that I can get quite upset when there are two people in my congregation that are complaining, but I forget that there are hundreds more right now who are not complaining. Be thankful for everything in your life that is going right. Count your blessings; name them one by one. That is not just a little kid's game; that is a spiritually mature adult reality. Every day we ought to be thanking God for his kind providence.

The beautiful thing about true thankfulness is that it too becomes an attitude of life. True thankfulness exerts itself as a fruit of daily conversion—the fruit of daily killing of sin and the daily quickening of the Holy Spirit. It is interesting that as the catechism goes on, it begins materially its section on true gratitude, the last section of the catechism, with the subject of what is true conversion. The answer is the mortification of the old man and the quickening of the new man. This is a daily experience requiring daily repentance. Daily taking refuge in Christ is rooted in daily thankfulness.

So, true thanksgiving is always rooted in three things. First, it is rooted in our daily repentance, confessing our own unworthiness, because then alone can we be thankful. Second, it is always Christ centered because it ends in our thanking the great High Priest with all the poverty of our own thanksgiving—because we are never as thankful as we ought to be. Third, it always ends in the Father, who gives the unspeakable gift of his own Son. In true thanksgiving we clasp his hand of mercy, and we glorify him for all that he bestows on us.

This true thanksgiving is also a strategy for our spiritual warfare against the world, the flesh, and the devil. Faith is always remembering to praise the Lord and to thank him for his benefits. As I have gone to different countries, I have noticed that certain groups of believers in different countries are much better at this than others. I was so moved at how the men in Northern Ireland pray. They adore God and thank him at the beginning of their prayers—sometimes going on for several minutes just telling God how wonderful he is and how grateful they are to be in his presence—before they even mention any supplication. This cultivates in their hearts a wonderful attitude of profound and deep thanksgiving to a triune God, so that we realize that we love and need each person of the Trinity. So, I am thankful for the Father and his electing love and providence; I am thankful for the Son and his redemption and constant intercession; I am thankful for the Holy Spirit and his patience in working in my soul the wonderful work of salvation.

Some people think it is much easier to be thankful in prosperity than to be patient in adversity. Both, however, are foreign to our natural hearts. Both are impossible for us by nature because we do not really see God's fatherly hand of providence stretched out toward us in either adversity or prosperity apart from the Spirit's grace. But when we do, we can be thankful for the smallest things in life.

How strange this response to prosperity is to the unbeliever. The natural non-Christian response to prosperity is pride and haughtiness. Moses prophesies that when the Israelites settle into the good land that their "thine heart be lifted up, and thou forget the LORD your God." They will say, "My power and the might of mine hand hath gotten me this wealth" (Deut 8:14, 17 KJV). They should be thankful in their prosperity and praise the Lord God for the good land he gave. VanderKemp calls this disregard for God's providence "a brutish stupidity, which does not look upward."[10] He compares such an ungrateful person to a brute—a beast. The beast does not acknowledge the hand that feeds it. When you drop pig feed into a trough, the pig does not look upward. It does not appreciate the giver. It is stupid, VanderKemp says, like the wicked, who are not thankful in prosperity. They are like animals that just take what comes their way without giving a single thought to the provider. God declares about such people, "Because they regard not the works of the LORD, nor the operation of his hands, he shall destroy them, and not build them up" (Ps 28:5).

Conversely, says Wilhelmus à Brakel, "The proper use of God's providence will render you an exceptional measure of gratitude and will teach you to end in the Lord as the only Giver of all the good which you may receive for soul and body."[11] This is the understanding that David has. When he recalls the Lord's providential benefits he exclaims, "Blessed be the Lord, who daily loadeth us with benefits, even the God of our salvation"

---

10. VanderKemp, *Christian Entirely the Property of Christ*, 1:226.

11. Wilhelmus à Brakel, *The Christian's Reasonable Service*, ed. Joel R. Beeke, trans. Bartel Elshout (Grand Rapids: Reformation Heritage Books, 1999), 1:53.

(Ps 68:19). Then we can be thankful for even the smallest things in life. I will never forget going to visit my father after his heart surgery. I found him weeping and I said, "Dad, what's wrong?"

He said, "Oh, I am just crying tears of thankfulness. A nurse just came in and moistened my lips with an ice cube, and as she left I was thinking about Luke 16, where the rich man had not a drop of water to cool his tongue. And who am I? I deserve the portion of the rich man in hell, and God sent that nurse in here to moisten my lips, and it felt so good." Have you ever thanked God for an ice cube?

Being thankful in prosperity is a work of true faith. But it is also a strategy for our spiritual warfare against the world, the flesh, and the devil. Faith remembers to praise the Lord and forgets not all his benefits. In doing so, faith protects us from hardness of heart, excess of pride, and indulgence in spiritual folly that would otherwise be fatal to us, if not now, then in the age to come. But there is one further advantage to believing in divine providence.

Facing the Future with Confidence in God

The third great advantage of faith in divine providence is facing the future with confidence in God. Of all people, Christians ought to be the most optimistic in the world. Knowing that God is our Father for the sake of Christ, his Son, means that we are loved with an everlasting love that cannot change, cannot wane or ebb, and cannot ever depart from us. Or, as the catechism says, "In all things which may hereafter befall us, we place our firm trust in our faithful God and Father, that nothing shall separate us from His love" (question 28; see Rom 8:38–39).

We must remember that the framers of the catechism lived in a time when suffering and death were a real possibility for Reformed Christians. If, for the moment, they enjoyed the favor and protection of a Reformed prince, there was every possibility that he might die and be succeeded by someone of a very different faith and inclination. Their kingdom was surrounded by others who were hostile to their Reformed convictions, and these powers could invade their borders, taking them captive and leading them to a fiery death. They had to reckon with the grimmest possibilities of what might befall them in the balance of their time on earth.

So, it is even more remarkable that they expressed their faith in God's providence in such absolute terms. They knew that everything depends on God. They believed that "all creatures are so in his hand, that without His will they cannot so much as move" (Heidelberg Catechism, Q. 28). That is about the best definition ever stated in plain language of what Calvinists mean by the sovereignty of God.

The English version says that we Christians should "place our firm trust in our faithful God and Father." "Firm faith" is a good translation, but it loses just a bit from the original statement in Dutch. More literally translated, the catechism says that we should "have a good expectation on" (*een goed toevoorzicht hebben op*) our faithful God and Father. That is to say, we Christians should live with great expectations, with a faith that knows well what we already have in Christ and anticipates fully all that is laid up in store for us and all that is sure to come to us in due time—if we hold fast our "confidence and the rejoicing of the hope firm unto the end" (Heb 3:6).

Only true, experiential faith in God will produce a calm, firm trust in God for the future. Trust in God is trusting in the Almighty, who has the whole world in his providential hands. The future may be unknown, but if we know the God of the future in Christ, we have everything. If I have faith in God's providential hand, I not only learn to *see* my Father's hand in ordinary events and to *feel* my Father's hand in adversity and prosperity, but I also learn to *hold* my Father's hand as I face the future. I learn to place my firm trust in our faithful God and Father, that nothing shall separate us from his love.

The catechism does not say, "No creature will ever cause us harm," but, "No creature will ever separate us from God's love!" Much can be taken from us, but the love of God shall never be taken away. That bond of love can never be severed.

That is what Romans 8 so powerfully proclaims. Those four couplets that Paul refers to at the end of Romans 8 represent all the things that we by nature fear will separate us from the love of God in Christ Jesus our Lord. "Death, nor life" (8:38). Death is separating, is it not? No, says Paul. Death is like a wheelchair that ushers us into Christ's presence into the celestial city where no wheel chairs will ever be needed again. It will not separate us; it will bring us closer to Jesus. But how about life—will that not separate me? No, says Paul. The busyness of life? No, says Paul. When you are very busy it will throw you even more on the Lord; you will need him more and more. What about angels, principalities, or powers? Angels or devils—they will not separate us from God's love. All the devils in hell cannot separate you, and that is because of the cross. They try to separate us. The devils thought they were getting the victory when Christ was dying, but he was crushing the head of the serpent. Even if an angel could come from heaven and preach another gospel, he would not separate you because the Holy Spirit is stronger than any angel.

Nothing "shall be able to separate us from the love of God" (Rom 8:39)—so we do not need to be anxious when rumors are spread or when dangers threaten. All that I am and all that I have is in my Father's hand. All I need is to take my Father's hand—to hold that strong, steady, guiding, unfailing hand, which will never let me go.

> In sweet communion Lord, with Thee
> I constantly abide
> My hand Thou holdest in Thy own
> To keep me near Thy side.[12]

When I was a bit younger and my children were small, there was a point at which I showed each of them the very busy road in front of our house. I put a chalk line on the driveway and said, "Do not ever go beyond this point by yourself." I got down on my knees and looked at them eyeball to eyeball and said, "Daddy will punish you if you ever try to walk across this road on your own. You could die if you do! Don't you ever try to go across this road on your own. I will spank you hard. Do you understand?" But could they ever make it to the road? No, my wife would have seen it, and she would have

---

12. In Joel Beeke, ed., *The Psalter* (Grand Rapids: Reformation Heritage Books, 1999), no. 203, stanza 1.

run out and stopped them before they made it to the road. But I used that warning to help prevent them from even wanting to go that way.

Sometimes, of course, we had to cross the road, so how did we do it? We took them by the hand, and when we got to the road I would say, "Now hold Daddy's hand tightly." I held their hand tightly as I commanded them to hold my hand tightly, and we would go across the road together. That is the way to face the future. You cannot go on your own. But you hold God's hand tightly because he holds you tightly, and you go forward in his love, trusting him that he will make all things well. That gives you security for every storm. As we traverse the highways and byways of this life, the Lord says, "Come, child, take my hand; hold my hand." Then he takes our hand and holds it tightly in his own. We hold on to him because he holds on to us. We cling to him because he clings to us. We love him because he first loved us. One day the bond of love will be drawn so tightly that we will be drawn into his eternal, loving presence. We shall see him forever and enjoy his love undisturbed.

The love of our heavenly Father in Christ Jesus—that is the *content* of our trust. That love, which is grounded in the Father's love for his own Son, is the surest guarantee; it is the greatest treasure. We can make ends meet without almost anything in this life—but we cannot miss this love.

This love gives childlike trust. It gives stability and freedom from fear. Think of your own children. Why are they so secure? Because they know you love them; they know you would do anything to do the best for them. You will protect them, with as much as in you lies, from every enemy and every hostile force. This gives them trust in you and in the future.

Much more so are God's children related to their Father in heaven. You can only protect your children to a certain degree. Our Father in heaven is in control of everything. He protects us perfectly. Question 28 of the catechism concludes, "All creatures are so in His hand that without His will they cannot so much as move." Those creatures can be strong, and they can cause us much grief, but they are totally impotent in the hands of our Father. Without his will they cannot so much as move. That is the *foundation* of our trust: our Father is in control of every storm.

The story is told of a boy on a ship in the middle of a severe storm. Most of the people were very afraid as the waves came over the ship, but they noticed how calm the boy was, and someone asked him, "Why aren't you afraid?" The boy said, "My father is the captain." Dear child of God, your Father commands the waves, and they are quiet. He speaks, and it is done. He commands, and all stands fast. He will bring you through every storm. That is what providence teaches you.

By nature, we are impatient and rebellious when things do not go as we want, proud when things go well, and anxious and fearful when thinking of an unknown future. This is natural, because fallen people sees themselves as the center of all things—as if they were God. What does not go according to my desires is most upsetting. What serves my honor and glory is most important, and what will happen in the future is in my weak hands—or it will be determined by unknowns such as more powerful people or forces. Therefore, I am fearful.

I need to tell myself that time and again. I am very worried about the direction of our nation. Our future, the advances of the gay lobby, terrorism—these things are very disturbing. Where will it all end? Will it end with the end of the world? Will our children be able to live to an age of retirement before the Lord Jesus comes on the clouds? How much depressing news there is locally, nationally, and internationally. That seems to be all we hear today.

But faith says that "God is king forever, let the nations tremble."[13] He is enthroned above the cherubim. His Son is set as the holy king on the hill of Zion. Yes, there may be rough times coming, but God is bigger than the times and bigger than the discouragements. We need to remind each other of that, because too often we act and react just like the world does to the events happening around us. We get just as upset as our neighbor who does not go to church. We complain nearly as much as the world does about the bad times in which we are living, and these complaints are too often sinful. No, we do not have to be immune to what is going on. Christians are not expected to be stoics, ones who never show emotion, so that no matter what

---

13. In Beeke, *Psalter*, no. 266, stanza 1.

happens to them they remain the same. That is not what a Christian is. Christians certainly may take these bad times to heart and may grieve over them, but they grieve in a different way than the world does.

When Daniel was at court in Babylon, he too was burdened with the events around him, especially as they related to Israel; but he brought these burdens to the Lord. He was affected by them, yet not as the world is affected by bad times. The world will grumble and complain, but the believer will take them to the Lord and will recognize that all this is happening because of sin. If you are a believer, you know that the difficult times our nation is going through are rooted in our sin—particularly in our lack of repentance and our unbelief. God is pouring his judgments on us—not, of course, nearly as much as we deserve, but he is pouring his judgments on us nonetheless. He is punishing the United States for departing from his word, and, therefore, we are going through difficult times. Does this drive you often to prayer for the well-being of the people and land we love so much? Do you intercede daily with God for the well-being of our nation?

All too often we react like the world and get upset. But Christians should not get upset. Christians should be able to rise above the circumstances around them. Show me a person who can say, Nothing can separate me from the love of God that is in Christ Jesus our Lord (Rom 8:38–39), and then you have shown me a Christian indeed. Do we have this faith? Or do we not dare to say what the catechism here says, that we place our firm trust, not just *once in a while*, but *habitually* in our faithful God and Father, that nothing shall separate us from his love—also not anything in the future? Let me summarize by asking this: How would your life be enriched more if you truly believed that the heavenly Father rules over all your personal thoughts, words, and actions, and all that happens to you?

You would live a more content, trusting life, placing your needs and cares in your Father's hand and leaving them with him. You would rest more in God with holy submission and gratitude. You would realize your dependency on God, keep your eye fixed on God, and walk more circumspectly. As children are completely dependent on their parents, clinging to the hand of their mother and living from the hand of their father, so you would live more by childlike faith, depending completely on God. You would have more patience in adversity, more thankfulness in prosperity, and more trust in God for the unknown future.

CONCLUSION: GLORIOUS LIBERTY

There is one glorious, biblical word that sums up all these advantages of believing in divine providence: liberty, the "glorious liberty of the children of God" (Rom 8:21). Freedom from fear of condemnation, fear of suffering and death, fear of want and shame, and fear of whatever the future holds; freedom from anxiety, worry, and the cares of this life; freedom from anything the world may threaten to do to us, anything the devil may wish to lay to our charge, and anything that may rise up against us in this life; freedom in Christ; freedom by faith—all this is the gift and entitlement conferred on us by God, who loves us now and will love us always, as our Father in heaven, for Christ's sake, and the mighty Upholder and Ruler of all the creatures of his hand.

Consequently, it is this precious doctrine of providence—providence viewed as flowing to us not merely from the left hand of God's forbearance, but flowing to us through the right hand of God's favor in Christ—that enables us who are true believers to cry out victoriously with Paul in the closing verses of Romans 8: "For I am persuaded, that neither death, nor life, nor angels, nor principalities, nor powers, nor things present, nor things to come, nor height, nor depth, nor any other creature, shall be able to separate us from the love of God, which is in Christ Jesus our Lord" (8:38–39).

So what is the conclusion of the providence of God? The conclusion is liberty, as I am bound to God. The psalmist puts it this way:

> I am Thy servant, bound yet free;
> Thy handmaid's son whose shackles Thou hast broken;
> Redeemed by grace, I will render as a token;
> My gratitude, my constant praise to Thee.[14]

---

14. In Beeke, *Psalter*, no. 426, stanza 9.

That is the way to live—bound yet free: bound to God, to his law, to his revealed will, to his sovereign will, and to his written will—bound to obedience, yet free, because he made me to live to his honor and glory. It is a glorious liberty to live to his honor and glory. There is freedom from anxiety, worry, and the cares of this life. There is freedom from anything the world may threaten to do to us and anything the devil might lay to our charge. There is freedom in Christ and freedom by faith. That is what believing in God's providence does for you.

FREEDOM OF INCLINATION AND ITS IMPLICATIONS FOR THE CHRISTIAN'S GROWTH IN SANCTIFICATION

BRUCE A. WARE

O ne area I believe can be profitably explored is the question of how believers might grow in making daily choices in their lives that would result in furthering their sanctification. Can we understand better just what role our choices make in growing in the Christian life? Is there a way to direct human choosing such that we grow in wanting the very things God wants us to want, and in turning aside from the very things God forbids? Why do we make the choices we do make, anyway? And is there a way to direct our pattern of choosing so that we increasingly resist choices that would lead us to what is either unprofitable or harmful, and increasingly embrace choices that promote growth in Christlike character and behavior?

I believe that there is help to be found on these and other such questions by understanding better the true nature of the human freedom God has given us, and then considering some of the implications this view of human freedom has for our growth in sanctification. I propose, then, to look first at just what our freedom is, using here what I consider to be the enormously insightful work of Jonathan Edwards. Although there is another widely held understanding of freedom—libertarian freedom—which both Edwards and most in the Reformed tradition reject, Edwards's view of human freedom as freedom of inclination (in contrast to a freedom of indifference, found in libertarian freedom) proves enormously illuminating and succeeds in explaining why we do what we do.[1] Second, we will explore just how this understanding of human freedom can be employed for the purpose of advancing Christian sanctification, reflecting very practically on what Christians might do to promote patterns of decision-making that enable them to grow in Christ.

THE NATURE OF HUMAN FREEDOM AS FREEDOM OF INCLINATION

A feature of our human experience we often refer to is our human free will. It seems that everyone understands that we possess human freedom, but just what it is can be difficult to pin down. I am deeply grateful to Jonathan Edwards (1703–58) for his careful analysis and explanation of human freedom. Edwards understood human volition as the expression of the mind choosing according to what the mind has settled on as the "good" that it most wants. He insists that a person always seeks to seize what is the greatest good available now of choosing. Thus, in making a choice, one's mind evaluates the options presented to it and eventually settles on what it most wants due to assessing that one specific thing as presenting the most desirable good (as one perceives it to be). Edwards refers to this understanding of human freedom variously, but one term that communicates well what he argues is freedom of inclination. That is, we are free now of our choice if and only if we are unconstrained or uncoerced in choosing what our minds have settled on as that which we most want, or according to our strongest desire, or according to our highest inclination.[2] Consider a few statements from Edwards in explaining the nature of true freedom:

---

1. I have discussed and critiqued this alternative view of human freedom, often referred to as libertarian freedom, in Bruce A. Ware, *God's Greater Glory: The Exalted God of Scripture and the Christian Faith* (Wheaton, IL: Crossway, 2004), 63–67, 85–95; and Ware, "The Compatibility of Determinism and Human Freedom," in *Whomever He Wills: A Surprising Display of Sovereign Mercy*, ed. Matthew M. Barrett and Thomas J. Nettles (Cape Coral, FL: Founders, 2012), 212–30.

2. See *FW* part I, section 5, for his discussion of true freedom being devoid of constraint.

"In every act of will there is an act of choice; that in every volition there is a preference, or a prevailing inclination of the soul." And again:

> So that in every act, or going forth of the will, there is some preponderation of the mind or inclination, one way rather than another; and the soul had rather have or do one thing, than another, or than not to have or do that thing; and that there, where there is absolutely no preferring or choosing, but a perfect continuing equilibrium, there is no volition.

And again: "It is sufficient to my present purpose to say, it is that motive, which, as it stands in view of the mind, is the strongest, that determines the will."[3]

Please observe several aspects of what Edwards is arguing. First, a person's choosing can only happen as the mind is aware of and considers various features of alternative choices. At the very least would be the alternatives to do or not do, to have or not have, to act or not act, regarding some thing. Second, it may well be the case that as the mind considers the alternatives presented to it, it may be attracted to more than one possible choice. That is, the mind might find two or more possible choices desirable and truly want or be inclined toward more than one object of its choice. Third, as one considers the possible alternative choices, the mind eventually settles on one of those alternatives, one choice, as that which the mind wants most. That is, the will is free in choosing when the mind has assessed just what choice is most highly desirable and then sets itself to choose just that instead of even other very desirable choices. As Edwards says, "It is that motive, which … is the strongest that determines the will."[4]

This last point deserves some additional explanation, both because of how important this idea is to the very nature of free will itself and because of the appeal we will later make to this idea in understanding how sanctification progresses. Edwards's understanding of free will is not

---

3. *FW* 140–41.
4. *FW* 141.

adequately represented merely by saying that we choose freely when we choose what we want, or what we desire, or according to our inclinations. The problem with saying only this is that in most of our choices, certainly in all our difficult choices and decisions, we face more than one, perhaps several, desirable options. It is exactly this reality that makes the decision particularly difficult.

Consider, if you will, the dieter standing in front of the dessert table. We can easily imagine our dieter having several different, even conflicting, and yes, strong, desires simultaneously. Let us assume he has been diligent at resisting foods that are not on his diet, so he surely would have the real and genuine desire to turn away from these desserts altogether in order to stay on his diet. But as he gazes on the variety of desserts offered, he sees some that have been among his favorites that he has enjoyed over the years. So, he may well have a strong desire for the luscious chocolate cake, along with a strong desire for the juicy marionberry pie, and for the extraordinarily fluffy cheesecake. As he contemplates these options, somehow his mind settles on one of these options as what he most wants, as what he desires most strongly, or what he is inclined most compellingly to do. How do we know that his mind settles on one choice only, the one he most wants? Answer: he acts in one way, choosing one among these choices, and the one choice and subsequent action expresses what he desires most.

Let us suppose that what our dieter has settled on as his highest inclination or strongest desire is to reach out and help himself to a piece of the marionberry pie. At that moment, he is free insofar as, with all the factors present before him—factors that include his being on a diet, along with several appealing dessert options, as well as innumerable other factors we cannot begin to enumerate (e.g., how recently he has eaten, who is with him at that moment, what size the dessert pieces are, etc.)—he acts according to what he most wants. For reasons that may not be easily understood, his mind settles on taking the marionberry pie as what he most wants, and he acts accordingly by reaching out to take a piece from off the table. But now suppose further that after he made this choice and is reaching out to pick up a piece of pie, at a distance behind him our dieter hears the voice of his wife approaching. Given this new factor, suddenly, his strongest desire changes. Since his wife has been so pleased with him that he has been consistent staying on his diet, he now has as his strongest desire something different from what had been his strongest desire just a few seconds earlier. Now, his mind settles on the choice of moving away from the dessert table, thus passing up all those delicious desserts, as that which he most wants, and he proudly announces to his wife, "They look delicious, but I don't want any of these tempting desserts." Of course, the truth is that he *does* want them; he especially wants a piece of the marionberry pie, which had been his strongest desire just a moment earlier. But as his wife approaches, he now wants most strongly to resist any and all those desserts in order to show her that he is staying on his diet.

The point is this: our freedom in choosing is expressed, now of settling on the choice we make, when our mind has considered all the desirable options available to us and it settles on just one of those options as that which accords with our *highest* inclination or *strongest* desire. That we do freely what we *most* want is central to the freedom of choice we have.

Besides considering these issues, Edwards also makes one additional very important point about the freedom of inclination he describes. Concerning this fourth feature, he writes: "Whatever is perceived or apprehended by an intelligent and voluntary agent, which has the nature and influence of a motive to volition or choice, is considered or viewed *as good*."[5] And again: "The will always is as the greatest apparent good is." And again: "And therefore that must have the greatest tendency to attract and engage it, which, as it stands in the mind's view, suits it best, and pleases it most; and in that sense, is the greatest apparent good: to say otherwise, is little, if anything, short of a direct and plain contradiction." And again:

> I think so much is certain, that volition, in no one instance that can be mentioned, is otherwise than the greatest apparent good is, in the manner which has been explained. The choice of the mind never departs from that which, at the time, and with respect to the direct and immediate objects

---

5. *FW* 142 (italics original).

of that decision of the mind, appears most agreeable and
pleasing, all things considered.[6]

What we have seen thus far is that true human freedom is expressed when
the mind considers the options before it and assesses them regarding which
choice and subsequent action accords with one's highest inclination, one's
strongest desire, or is more simply what one most wants. A person's motive,
then, is displayed when one discerns just what it is that one prefers above
all other available choices. This is true as far as it goes. But one significant
question has yet to be asked: What is it about the choice that one wants most
that elicits in the mind its assessment that this one thing alone (of possible
choices available to it) is to be preferred? Just why does one settle on one
thing over others as one's highest desire?

Edwards's answer here is simple yet profound. What one always desires
above all other choices available to it is that singular choice that, all things
considered, provides the *greatest apparent good* to the subject choosing. Notice
that Edwards is not saying that we always choose what is in fact the greatest
real good available now of choice; rather, we choose what we perceive
contains the greatest measure of good, as it appears to the mind. So, why
do we most want what we do and so act accordingly? Answer: we most want,
and so act, based on what we perceive to contain the greatest good out of
all the choices available to us at the time.

It should be apparent from this discussion how beautifully Edwards's
freedom of inclination accounts for why we do what we do, why we make
the choices we make, and why we carry out the actions we perform. Of the
choices available to us at any given time, we are free insofar as the mind is
uncoerced in assessing what apparent goods might inhere in each of these
various possible choices. Difficult choices are difficult precisely because some
perceived good obtains in several choice options. As the mind assesses, it
eventually settles on the one choice which it perceives will bring the greatest
good at that moment, given the present range of possible choices. So, that we
do freely what we *most want*, and that we most want what the mind perceives

---

6. *FW* 142–43, 147.

as containing the *greatest good* among choices available—these are central to understanding the nature of human freedom as a freedom of inclination.

FREEDOM OF INCLINATION AND PATTERNS OF CHOOSING THAT PROMOTE SANCTIFICATION

If one has been following the flow of the discussion above, I hope the implications for Christian sanctification are already becoming apparent. In brief, what we need to see in order to apply this understanding of human freedom to growing in Christlikeness are these two things: First, if we always do what we most want, then we need to consider how to *grow in most wanting* what we should (i.e., what God wants us to) most want. Second, if our mind's assessment of what it most wants is based on the perceived good in the alternative options before us at any given time, then we need to consider how to *grow in discerning the real good* from the merely perceived good in the various possible choices before us. Only as we grow in these two areas will we see significant changes in the patterns of our choosing, and hence in the transformation that takes place in our inner lives and outward behavior as believers. In what follows, consider just how we can make progress in both areas and through this see a way forward, if only dimly, in changes that are sanctifying of our lives.

First, how do we *grow in most wanting* what we should (i.e., what God wants us to) most want? I am quite aware that others will be able to answer this question in ways that add to and even surpass anything I might suggest here. But I hope and pray that the few thoughts presented here may be of some real and tangible assistance.

Where we need to begin is in assessing first the kind of nature we have as those created in the image of God, fallen due to sin, yet redeemed in Christ. Our natures when created were able to obey God consistently, as evidenced by the fact that Adam and Eve always wanted most to do what God wanted them to do (i.e., they never sinned until the sin of Gen 3). But this changed, of course, when sin entered the picture. Due to the deception and lies that Satan used, they believed the lie and so turned away from God. That is, for the first time they most wanted to go against God's will, believing (wrongly) that this would prove to advance their good (more on this shortly). Because we are "in Adam," we are fallen, and in this fallen state apart from God's grace in Christ, every one of our strongest inclinations and desires, every moment of our fallen and unsaved experience, shows that we "fall short of the glory of God" (Rom 3:23) in that we do not want truly to honor God, to thank God (Rom 1:21), or to please God (Rom 8:7–8).

In this fallen condition, though we can never do what God would approve in that our natures are bound to choose and act sinfully in one form or another, still our free will functions as it always has and always will, in that we do what we most want. It is just that as fallen sinners and apart from saving grace, we always have as our highest desire to sin, one way or the other. When we are saved by God's grace, through faith, we begin anew to have desires to please God and to do his will. Yet, we are not yet perfect and so we sometimes most want to obey, and sadly we also sometimes most want to disobey God's good and perfect will. In our lives now as Christians, we find a struggle, as Paul describes in Galatians 5. Our flesh wars against the Spirit and the Spirit against our flesh. When our flesh wins out, we choose and act in ways that show we most want to go our own way and turn from God. But when we walk in the Spirit, we choose and act in ways that show that we most want to do what pleases God. Again, the common feature here, as with the full range of our experience as human beings, is that we always do what we most want.

Given that we, as Christians, always choose and act in accordance with our highest inclinations and strongest desires, the key question becomes this: How can we promote inclinations and desires within that are in keeping with God's character and God's will, inclinations and desires that grow in strength over time so that eventually these godly desires become our highest desires? In other words, how can we grow in wanting most what God wants us to want most?

In answer to this important question, I suggest that here is exactly where the disciplines of the Christian life come to our aid. Don Whitney's discussion of the spiritual disciplines demonstrates that these disciplines should be seen (among other things) as supporters and strengtheners to our deepest Spirit-wrought desires so that these desires grow in wanting more strongly what God wants and commands us to do. Disciplines such as consistent time in God's word, prayer, worship, evangelism, serving, stewardship, fasting, regular submission to the preached word, and fellowship of the church gathered—these and more provide instruction, incentive, and motivation for growing in wanting more and more what God wants us to desire.

Much could be said about each one of these disciplines, but for the sake of space, allow me to develop more fully only one of these, that is, how our reading of God's word may strengthen our desires to follow God and his ways so that we increasingly become those who desire most strongly to trust and obey God's will, God's word, and God's ways.[7] Consider with me five practical aspects of a growing and healthy approach to the intake of God's word.

First, commit yourself to consistent Bible reading. Since the word of God written (Scripture) is the main instrument God has provided his people to know his character, to know his plans and purposes, to know his work in creation and redemption, to know ourselves, and to know how we are to live before him and others, it only stands to reason that we need regular time in God's word for that word to affect our lives. Consistency, rather than haphazardness, should mark our reading of Scripture. Of course, we all know that emergencies arise and life's messes interrupt. But it is one thing to have a few stop-outs in an otherwise consistent Bible reading plan; it is another simply to read only when it is convenient to do so. Because it is hard to exaggerate the importance of God's word to the formation of our minds, hearts, and lives (e.g., meditate on 2 Tim 3:16–17 and see what I mean), and because that word will only have its greatest potential impact as we read it regularly, please consider making consistency a mark of your Bible reading approach.

Second, engage in both fast-paced and slow-paced Bible reading. I am convinced that every Christian would benefit much more from their reading of God's word if they would train themselves in two very different forms of reading Scripture. Fast-paced reading is necessary if we are to cover the whole of the Scriptures at regular interval. It does not have to be a "read

---

7. There is no better source to see these developed than Donald S. Whitney, *Spiritual Disciplines of the Christian Life* (Colorado Springs: NavPress, 1991; rev. ed., 2014).

the Bible in a year" program, necessarily, but I would hope each of us would commit to reading every single book and chapter of the Bible at least every two or three years. Even at that pace, it requires that we keep moving and not get too bogged down. Perhaps here you might consider listening to the Bible read to you (as available online with several different translations) so that the Bible reader will keep you moving. To cover the whole ground of the Bible, we need to read the Bible in a fast-paced manner. Slow-paced reading, on the other hand, is necessary if we are to soak in and glory in the beauty and texture of so many passages of Scripture. Consider with me: if you only read, say, the book of Isaiah in a fast-paced manner, how much time will you devote to thinking about the substance of Isaiah 40, for example? Answer: about three minutes total, perhaps in a year, or two, or three. Yet, Isaiah 40 is rich with glorious teaching about God, about his work in creation and providence and redemption, and implications for the ways in which we should live our lives, that can only be seen and felt and marveled at when we read it slowly, prayerfully, meditatively, over and over and over. So, in addition to your fast-paced Bible reading, I would recommend that you consider taking some key portions of Scripture to meditate on over and over for a period of weeks, until you are confident you have seen more of the intricacies and beauty and wonder of those passages. Often, the most life-transforming aspects of the truth of God's word come in details that will only be apparent when we stop to smell the roses, as it were. Perhaps you could plan to read your fast readings four days a week, and then meditate over small units of Scripture the other two or three days a week. In any case, be assured of this. Both types of reading are important, and each yields a different kind of fruit for the Christian's life.

Third, notice the "who" as much, or more than, the "what" in your Bible reading. Never forget that there is one author of Scripture who stands over and above all the human authors of all the various books of Scripture—"All Scripture is breathed out by God," says Paul (2 Tim 3:16 ESV), and "Men moved by the Holy Spirit spoke from God," writes Peter (2 Pet 1:21 NASB). Since the Scriptures are the self-revelation of God himself, our focus when reading Scripture should be to encounter the author who is unfolding before us in the pages of Scripture something of his character and work through every book of the Bible. And, since the one God of Scripture is none other than the triune God of the Christian faith, pay special attention to what is revealed about the Father, and the Son, and the Holy Spirit as you read your Bible.

While it is important to learn what the Bible teaches each step along the way, throughout the whole of the Scriptures, even more important is coming to a clearer and brighter and richer and deeper understanding of who the true and living God is who stands behind and within all of Scripture. Grow in not just knowing more about God but grow in knowing God as you read your Bible. Focus on his attributes, his actions, his stated plans and purposes, his commandments and warnings, and his promises and his assurances. Knowing God is the great good for which we are created (e.g., Jer 9:23–24; John 17:3), and so intend every day, as you read your Bible, to know God better in every passage you read.

Fourth, seek both informed minds and stirred affections in your Bible reading. God intends the truth of his word to travel, as it were, first into our minds, but then from our minds to our hearts. We are to know the truth of God's word, indeed. But we also are to see the beauty, and marvel at the richness, of that word. In short, we must grow, through our reading of Scripture, in knowing (mind) and loving (heart) the glorious truths we encounter along the way. I would recommend that you consider pledging yourself to praying each time before your read your Bible, "Lord, in your mercy and kindness, open your word to me, and open me to your word."

The first request has mostly to do with our minds, as we ask for Spirit-given illumination to know accurately what God's word teaches. But the second part of this simple prayer has mostly to do with our hearts, as we seek that same Spirit to awaken within us an effective response to his word, where we feel the challenge, and see the wonder, and respond with our affections to the glory of the truth we have come to see. I believe it to be a dangerous pattern for Christians to read God's word consistently without having their hearts stirred by what is encountered. I suggest endeavoring never to finish your time in God's word without having at least one truth move your affections. So, if you finish your Bible reading and nothing has moved your heart, pray and ask God to show you one little thing from what you have read that can have an impact on your affections. Let that truth convict, or encourage, or correct, or strengthen hope, or embolden action—seek, before the Lord, at least one truth that will engage your heart's response. Since changed affections are the key to changed lives, may we prayerfully seek not only knowledge of God's word, but love for the beauty, wonder, and glory of that word.

Fifth, commit yourself to hear and heed, understand and obey, what you encounter in your Bible reading. James' powerful reminder that we are to be doers, and not merely hearers, of God's word (Jas 1:22) must be central in our thinking every day as we read the Scriptures. Since we are not our own, since we have been bought with a price (1 Cor 6:19–20), we must acknowledge we are under the lordship of our Savior Jesus every day, in every way possible. So, to read the word of God is to take up that which instructs how we are to live day by day. Let us resist the temptation to have minds growing in the knowledge of God's word that nonetheless fail to live out the truth of what we have come to know. Again, here is where some of the importance of the previous point comes to bear: we are changed in our behavior not principally in what we know, but in what we love and hate, in what we cherish or despise. So, indeed, God does intend this truth to travel, but there is one more destination point we must recognize. God intends his truth to travel first into our heads, then to our hearts, and then from our hearts through our hands. How we live is largely a reflection of changed affections. Let us never forget, then, that we are called by God to hear and heed, to understand and then to obey, the glorious, life-giving word he has provided for us.

Given these five aspects of how a Christian may approach the reading of God's word, it should be evident how each of these provides pathways of instruction, incentive, prodding, encouragement, admonition, correction, and marveling—all of which can be used by the Spirit to produce within us deepened desires to trust and obey God and his word. To have and experience what God most wants for us, we must likewise most want the same things. Surely devotion to the word of God is one essential aspect in moving our hearts and affections to desire above all to follow God faithfully.

Second, if our mind's assessment of what it most wants is based on the perceived good in the alternative options before us at any given time, then we need to consider how to *grow in discerning the real good* from the merely perceived good in the various possible choices before us. If we are bringing into our lives those stimuli that grant to us deepened desires to trust and obey God, then surely one other thing is also true: we are seeing God's word and ways as truly and genuinely for our good. If, on the other hand, we are engaging in the disciplines of the Spirit, such as regular Bible reading and prayer, yet we simply are not developing stronger desires to resist temptation and to obey God's word, then the problem is, at its root, a failure to see the will and ways and word of God as the only true good that there is. We have been deceived by Satan, as Adam and Eve were, to think that our true good is found by going our own way, living as we please. So, how can we grow in seeing the ways of God as constituting the true (and only) good for our lives now and forevermore?

Let me suggest here both a negative and a positive approach to assessing where the true good lies among the alternative choices before us at any given moment. Negatively, we should study carefully the deceptiveness of Satan and his attractions, in which he seeks to convince us that his way, not God's, is the true pathway to our good. We must remember that he is a liar and the father of lies (John 8:44). When he successfully tempts such that we succumb to that temptation, he has deceived us into thinking wrongly that the path of sinful disregard of God is good. In other words, we have been duped! We have been made the fool!

So, how can we grow in seeing his temptations for what they are—as deceptively offered pathways promising good but delivering harm and destruction? We will benefit as we think more clearly about the wiles of Satan and the kinds of strategies he employs. Here I would recommend two books that provide enormous insight into the deceptive schemes of the devil: C. S. Lewis's *The Screwtape Letters*, and Thomas Brooks's *Precious Remedies against Satan's Devices*.[8] Both provide invaluable insights into the methods and

---

8. C. S. Lewis, *The Screwtape Letters* (New York: Macmillan, 1962); Thomas Brooks, *Precious Remedies against Satan's Devices* (1718; repr. Edinburgh: Banner of Truth Trust, 1981).

mindset of Satan in his endeavors to trip us up. Learning more about the strategies of the enemy can provide clarity and focus on where the good in life truly is, and it surely is not in the deceptive and destructive pathways of Satan but always and only with God.

Positively, we must pursue God in Christ with greater zeal and longing. I recall reading many years ago the famous sermon by Thomas Chalmers titled "The Expulsive Power of a New Affection."[9] Chalmers's main claim is that we never will successfully develop the kinds of desires for godliness necessary only by the defensive means noted above. If we endeavor to push sin out of our lives, trying to convince ourselves how bad it is, we will inevitably turn to it again. That negative strategy, as important as it is, must be coupled with a positive strategy. Positively, we must bring into our lives new affections that are deeper, richer, more glorious, and more deeply satisfying than our affections were for sin. When new and stronger affections enter, they push out the old ones; hence, the expulsive power of a new affection.

The apostle Paul certainly practiced this principle, as recorded in Philippians 3. Recall that he writes, "I count all things to be loss in view of the *surpassing value* of knowing Christ Jesus my Lord, for whom I have suffered the loss of all things, and count them but rubbish so that I may gain Christ" (Phil 3:8 NASB). Notice that those "all things" that he now counts as loss used to be the things he lived for; they provided him his sense of significance, satisfaction, and joy. But now, since he has come to know Christ, these other, lesser realities simply get pushed out. The surpassing value of knowing Christ makes all else look pale in contrast to the true splendor, beauty, and goodness found in Christ.

So, how can we grow in detecting where true goodness is found? We must grow in seeing the temptations and allurements of this life for the deceptive realities that they are, offering happiness and goodness but delivering always, without fail, what disappoints, harms, and will ultimately

9. Thomas Chalmers, *The Expulsive Power of a New Affection* (Minneapolis: Curiosmith, 2012), available online at https://www.monergism.com/thethreshold/sdg/Chalmers,%20Thomas%20-%20The%20Exlpulsive%20Power%20of%20a%20New%20Af.pdf (accessed November 1, 2018).

destroy, if continued to the end. Along with this strategy, we must pursue the "surpassing value" of Christ and the true good offered us in God's word and God's ways. We must believe Jesus when he says that he came that we might "have life and have it abundantly" (John 10:10 NASB). Here is true beauty and goodness, and here alone.

CONCLUSION

Without question, one of the most important observations of human life was made by Edwards when he noted that our freedom functions in such a way that we always choose and act according to our strongest inclinations, our deepest desires, or what we most want. Further, what we most want turns out to be the outworking of our mind's assessment of where we believe real good lies. God made us to long for good (since he made us to long for him, who alone is good!), and we trip and fall when we wrongly think good is found anywhere contrary to God and his ways. May God work within us, by his word and Spirit, to undertake the regular and practiced training in righteousness called for in order to develop increasing desires to trust and obey God. As we do this, may God receive the honor he alone deserves as we experience the only true joy that there is. For God's glory and our good, may we desire him most and above all.

PRESSING ON

Remaining Steadfast in the Pursuit of Christ

STEVEN J. LAWSON

Not that I have already obtained it or have already become
perfect, but I press on so that I may lay hold of that for which
also I was laid hold of by Christ Jesus. Brethren, I do not
regard myself as having laid hold of it yet; but one thing I do:
forgetting what lies behind and reaching forward to what lies
ahead, I press on toward the goal for the prize of the upward
call of God in Christ Jesus.

—Philippians 3:12–14

A SOLDIER, A FARMER, A STUDENT

These tangible images are often used to describe the Christian life. Several metaphors appear in Scripture to represent the life of the believer. Images such as that of a farmer stress the importance of sowing the good seed. Others, such as the picture of a soldier, highlight the crucial nature of fighting the good fight. Many other key metaphors run through Scripture to describe a believer's identity, including that of a citizen, son, and bride.

In Philippians 3, Paul uses the vivid metaphor of an athlete. This picture is prominent in the New Testament and powerfully purposeful. Paul draws attention to the straining, pressing on, and intense focus of an athlete running the race of faith.

As believers, we are each like a runner in a race. The starting line is the new birth, the track is the will of God, and the rules are the word of God. The requirement is obedience to those rules from the heart, and the progress is spiritual growth. The ultimate prize at the end of the race is Jesus Christ himself—full knowledge of Christ, full conformity to him, and full pleasure in him.

This image is precisely how Paul represents what it is to be a believer. Paul writes these verses in an autobiographical way, as he uses himself as an example to instruct us in the Christian life.

Some time ago, one of the major seminaries in the United States surveyed its students upon their graduation. After four years of being taught systematic theology, Greek and Hebrew exegesis, and Bible exposition, the students were asked this question: "What is the one thing that was most lacking in your education?" Again and again the answer was simply this: "How do I live the Christian life?" With all this knowledge and information regarding the truth, there was still a struggle to know how to put it into practice and live it out. We all want a clear focus on how to live the Christian life. Philippians 3:12–14 paints a vivid picture for us, describing how to do just that.

THE SOBER ASSESSMENT (PHILIPPIANS 3:12A)

In Philippians 3:12, Paul writes, "Not that I have already obtained it."[1] What is the "it" Paul has not yet obtained? Paul writes in verse 10, "that I may know Him and the power of His resurrection and the fellowship of His sufferings, being conformed to His death."

In this passage, Paul realizes he has not yet fully emptied himself like Christ did when he laid aside his prerogatives as God to assume the form of a bondservant (Phil 2:7). Paul has not yet humbled himself to the lowest degree, like Christ did when he left the heights of heaven and came down into this world. Paul realizes he has not yet attained obedience unto death,

---

1. Unless otherwise stated, all Scripture quotations in this chapter conform to the NASB.

as Jesus did when he went to the cross (Phil 2:8). Paul fully acknowledges he has not arrived yet—he is still a work in process.

This is an amazing statement to come from the apostle! We could say the apostle Paul was the greatest Christian who ever lived. Yet Paul, the seemingly greatest Christian, says, "I have not attained it. I am not there yet." If it was true for Paul, how much more so is it true for us? We are all nowhere near where we need to be in our Christian growth and development. There is still so much more of Christ to experience in our own personal lives. The closer we draw to Christ, the more we realize we have not obtained spiritual perfection.

Paul gives a second denial as he writes, "or have already become perfect" (3:12). Paul once thought he was blameless before God. He was so self-deceived as a Pharisee, he thought he had arrived in his relationship with God. He thought he was a spiritual elitist and that he had surpassed everyone else in Israel.

In Philippians 3:5–6, Paul gives an impressive spiritual pedigree. From a human standpoint, he had everything—the right beginning, right nationality, right family pedigree, right upbringing, right standard, right passion, and right morality.

But once he came face-to-face with the risen Christ, he suddenly realized how far he had fallen short of God's glory. Paul had assumed he had arrived as a Pharisee until he met the ultimate standard—the Lord Jesus Christ himself. He was no longer comparing himself with someone else in Israel who was a little bit behind him in his Pharisaism. When he met Christ, he compared himself to incarnate deity, and his only conclusion was that he was the chief of sinners (see 1 Tim 1:15). Seeing the perfect righteousness of Christ suddenly shattered his self-righteousness. In that instant, he counted all things he once trusted to make him right before God as complete and utter loss. He knew he fell far short of the perfection of Christ, just as we all have.

As Paul now lives his Christian life, he realizes he has only just begun the race to pursue Christ. In fact, the closer he draws to the finish line, the more he realizes how far short he still falls (see Rom 7). This is where we must find ourselves. We have not yet arrived, not by a long shot. None of us should be on a spiritual plateau. None of us can sit back and be content with where we are right now. There is still so much more of Jesus Christ for us to follow, emulate, trust, believe, and become like. If Paul says this of himself, how much more so does this apply to us?

THE STRENUOUS EFFORT (PHILIPPIANS 3:12B)

When Paul realized how far behind he was in the race to Christlikeness, it motivated him to press all the more to become like his Savior. Paul writes, "But I press on." "Press on" (*diōkō*) is a Greek word that literally means "to move rapidly and decisively after an object." It is to run after something swiftly, as you would to catch another person. I remember running track and having another runner out ahead of me, and the feeling of the baton being placed in my hand. It motivated me to run faster than if I had the lead. *I need to catch this person before I hand off the baton to the next runner—no matter what.* That determination is what Paul is feeling here, as he knows that Christ is so far out ahead of him.

Diōkō is the same word used in 3:6, when Paul says he was a "persecutor" of the church. A persecutor is someone who runs after Christians in order to apprehend, lay hold of, and drag them before the tribunal, like Stephen when he was stoned to death. Paul uses the same tenacity he once had to run after Christians to now run after Christ. Such was the tremendous shift in his heart and life.

Paul had always run swiftly in his life. Even when he was going in the wrong direction, he was running full tilt. Once he met Christ and his life was radically turned around, that same energy and zeal was now fueled by the Holy Spirit and a vision of who Christ is. He now runs as fast as his spiritual stamina will take him after Christ.

Paul pictures himself as a runner, widening his stride in prayer and pumping his arms in the study of Scripture. He accelerates his legs in worship. He pushes out his chest in ministry. He expends every ounce of energy within him, making every effort to press on to spiritual maturity. He labors to the point of exhaustion in his spiritual life, holding nothing back, leaving it all on the track of life. Paul provides a model for pursuing the person of Jesus Christ, keeping pace with the rhythm of godly living.

Paul continues and says, "So that I may lay hold of that for which I was also laid hold of by Christ Jesus" (3:12). He gives a cause and effect at the end of verse 12, and the effect is stated before the cause. The cause is that Paul was laid hold of by Jesus Christ. In other words, Jesus sought him, Jesus found him, Jesus ran him down. Paul was not looking for Jesus. Instead, Paul was running after Christians to persecute them. Jesus Christ, the Lord of heaven and earth, appeared to Paul, ran him down, laid hold of him, sovereignly apprehended him, and brought him into the kingdom of heaven.

Paul now desires to lay hold of Christ like Christ once laid hold of him. Jesus was so powerful and so full of dynamism in his pursuit of Paul that Paul now gives his whole life to run after the one who ran after him.

There is nothing passive about the Christian life. There is no "let go and let God." Paul is not sitting back and waiting for something to happen in his life. There is no dismissal of obedience, no downplaying of his personal responsibility, no antinomianism. There is no looking back to his justification and assuming he has arrived spiritually. On the contrary, Paul runs with all the strength God gives him to run after and pursue the Lord Jesus Christ. The Christian life requires an all-out effort in spiritual disciplines to cultivate personal holiness.

Using the same athletic metaphor, Paul writes elsewhere, "Run in such a way that you may win" (1 Cor 9:24). We are commanded to run, not sit or shuffle. Pursue victory! Run! Paul later writes, "I run in such a way, as not without aim; I box in such a way, as not beating the air; but I discipline my body and make it my slave" (1 Cor 9:26–27). An athlete tells his body what to do. An athlete tells his body when to wake up, what to eat, when to work out, and when to go to sleep. He is not sitting back just waiting for a feeling. When I played college football, the coaching staff told me when I would wake up, when I would go to sleep, when I would show up for practice, and when I would show up for training. That is the way an athlete lives his life—with all-out discipline. Christians must live their lives with the same dedication.

We are called to be active—resist temptation, flee immorality, fight the good fight. We must be diligent to present ourselves as workers who need not be ashamed. We must discipline ourselves for the purpose of godliness. We must labor and strive. In 1 Timothy 4:10, the word "labor" (*kopios*) means to push yourself to the point of exhaustion until you have no energy left. It is as if they must carry you off the field because you have given your all in the pursuit of victory. The Greek word for "strive" is *agōnizomai*, where we get the word "agonize." This is part of what it is to live the Christian life. We must work out our salvation in fear and trembling, pray without ceasing, and cry out for the pure milk of the word. Many of these phrases are imperatives—divine commands to pick up our pace, widen our stride, and to press on in this pursuit of Christlikeness.

Be diligent to discipline yourself for godliness. Buffet your body and make it your slave. Bring your life into submission in spiritual disciplines like Bible study, Bible reading, prayer, corporate and individual worship, fellowship, ministry, evangelism, and missions. In the word of God, you must read, study, internalize, obey, live, speak, and spread it. In prayer, you must worship God, confess sin, make petitions, intercede for others, and express thanks. These are all parts of running the race God has for us.

THE SINGULAR FOCUS (PHILIPPIANS 3:13)

Great runners must keep their eyes on the prize. Paul writes, "Brethren, I do not regard myself as having laid hold of it yet" (Phil 3:13). Here, Paul repeats what he said in verse 12. Again, "it" refers to the full knowledge of Christ. Second Peter 3:18 says we are to "grow in the grace and knowledge of our Lord and Savior Jesus Christ." This "it" refers to complete conformity to Christ. There is so much more of Christ that must be manifested in our life, attitudes, actions, reactions, speech, and priorities. We must pursue this conformity with zeal.

The word "regard" (*logizomai*) refers to a mathematical calculation. As Paul does the math, it becomes clear that this is not an emotional reaction, and this is not Paul being melancholy. Paul makes a very careful calculation about who Christ is and where he is in his own spiritual life. Paul says in a very sane, realistic self-diagnosis of his own spiritual life, "I do not regard myself as having laid hold of it yet."

Paul then counters, "But one thing I do" (3:13). Not two things or three things—there is only one thing on Paul's agenda. Everything else takes a distant second. One thing rises to the top to dominate his life. One supreme goal, one highest priority, one overriding ambition demands his full and undivided attention—his total concentration. What is this one thing? Paul gives a negative denial and a positive assertion.

The negative denial is "forgetting what lies behind" (3:13). "Forgetting" (*epilanthanomai*) means "to put out of your mind." Any runner knows you cannot look back if you are going to run as fast as you can possibly run. Runners who look back risk being passed or tripped up. Looking back means potentially veering off the track or being disqualified. Runners are laser-focused on the finish line, unconcerned with whatever is behind them. In his spiritual race, Paul could easily look back to past sins, failures, tragedies, hurts, defeats, and victories. He could easily recollect his misspent years in dead religion, entangled in legalism and self-righteousness. But some of the things that slow us down the most are not our defeats, but our victories. In prosperity and ease, we begin to cruise, slow down, and stop pushing and stretching toward the finish line.

Jesus says in Luke 9:62, "No one, after putting his hand to the plow and looking back, is fit for the kingdom of God." There is no rearview mirror as we run the race. Some believers need to stop carrying things around from their past. It is over. It is no longer your burden to bear. Put it under the blood of Christ. Confess whatever sin there is and, by the grace of God, forget what lies behind and press forward to what lies ahead. Even the pain of past suffering should not hinder our pursuit of Christ but propel us further down the track.

The positive assertion at the end of verse 13 reads, "reaching forward to what lies ahead." "Reaching forward" (*epekteinomai*) is one word in the original language. The root means "to stretch." There is not just one but two prefixes in front of the main verb. This is like a double intensification of this stretch forward. These two prefixes are "out" and "upon." "Reaching forward" most literally means "to stretch out," as if to lay your hand upon, stretching as far as you can ahead of you. You are holding nothing back, you are stretching out to the limits in your pursuit of Jesus Christ, to know him, to become like him, to walk with him, and to run with him. It is straining every spiritual muscle.

We all need to be more highly motivated and better disciplined in our Christian lives. We should not be so content with where we are and what we know at this moment. Paul does not sit back. Paul disregards what lies behind, even forgetting how they laid the robes at his feet when they stoned Stephen to death. He is reaching forward to what lies ahead— Jesus Christ himself.

Where are you in your Christian life? What do you need to let go? What baggage do you need to discard? What past failures? What past sins? How do you need to reach forward with greater effort in your spiritual life? How do you need to pick up the pace? How do you need to better discipline yourself and the use of your time for maximum return in the Christian life? This is what Paul calls believers to—to pick up the pace and pursue Christ with everything they have.

THE SWIFT PACE (PHILIPPIANS 3:14)

Paul kept a swift pace. He continues, "I press on toward the goal for the prize" (Phil 3:14). Paul already said "I press on" in verse 12. To repeat it in verse 14 is to underscore the idea in our thinking. Remember, it means "to run swiftly in order to catch a person." It is in the present tense, meaning Paul is always pressing on. He fixes his eyes to the end of the race and allows that to direct his every move. He does not look to the right or left, does not look backward or over his shoulder, but his gaze is set straight ahead. This is not just a Sunday morning thing. This is not just a Thursday morning men's Bible study or a Thursday afternoon women's fellowship group. This is every moment of every day. Paul is continually pressing on. It is in the active voice, which means Paul bears personal responsibility to press on under the direction of the Holy Spirit. For Paul, there is no slowing down. He only picks up his speed as he runs the race.

The preposition "toward" (*kata*) means "down." The idea is that Paul is bearing down toward the goal. Paul moves toward the goal with intensity. "Goal" simply means "a mark" or "a target." Paul has a goal fixed before his eyes, and he strives for the prize. His prize is "the upward call of God in Christ Jesus" (3:14). Paul has already been called to Christ on earth, but this "prize" is a call to Christ in heaven. This is the upward call, as he will be pulled up into heaven at the time of his death or at the time of Christ's return. As he comes to the end of his life, Paul can just see the finish line in front of him. At that finish line, he sees the Lord Jesus Christ, the reward of his completion. It is pulling him forward and empowering him, by the Spirit of God, to keep on keeping on. To not let anything slow him down. To overcome whatever other obstacles are in his path. Being in Christ is the only basis by which anyone can be called upward into the glory of heaven. This is the finish line of the race of faith. This is where the prize will be realized. This is where Christ is, ready to receive Paul—and all who put their trust in Jesus.

When Paul receives this upward call, he is determined that he will not be shuffling down the track. He will not be sitting on the bench or be a spectator in the stands. Rather, he is sprinting at full speed to the finish line. He is on the track, running faster than he has ever run in his life in response to this upward call. The prize and treasure is Christ. Paul had entered the fullness of a relationship with Christ when he started the race, when he was born again. But now he looks with expectation to enter the very presence of Christ and to be glorified into his likeness. To know him with a greater height and depth and breadth and length than he has ever known Christ before. To know he will spend all eternity with Christ, and it will have made every sacrifice and every discipline worthwhile as he now enters the reward.

Are you in the race of faith? Have you been born again? If you are in the race, are you pressing on? Are you forgetting what lies behind? Do you have a singular focus on what lies ahead? Are you reaching out to the fullness of your faith to grow in the grace and knowledge of the Lord Jesus Christ? There is no greater joy and pleasure in life than to be making this advancement, as you mature and develop in your faith. But be certain, it will require maximum effort fueled by the Holy Spirit to reach that for which God has prepared for you. Our growth in grace requires our aggressive effort all the way to the end.

Sprint with your chest out, knees pumping, arms moving, pressing on to the finish. And there, at the end of your race, will be the great and glorious prize of Jesus Christ himself.

THE INTEGRITY OF THE LOCAL CHURCH

JIM ELLIFF

A protracted meeting was held in Eatonton, Georgia, 1837. A few people had been converted, and soon the church gathered by the river for baptism. One of the persons being baptized was a teenage girl. Her name was Caroline, or Carrie for short. Carrie had come to Christ with a great deal of conviction. She said in her own testimony, "I desire to be even more devoted to my Savior than I have ever been to the world." This, as we will see, was an intense desire. There at the riverside was one of her friends who was yet unconverted, named Julia. Julia, in fact, had been very close to Carrie in all kinds of worldly exploits. So this unsaved girl was now watching the baptism of her closest friend. Somebody recorded the event in what I think is rather eloquent terminology:

> Of course everybody was there. The banks of that little stream were lined with crowds of interested spectators. … Julia, of Monticello, her bosom friend and companion in her worldly course, seemed loathe to leave her even for a moment and clung to her till she reached the water's edge. A hymn was sung and [minister C. D.] Mallory made a few remarks and offered prayer, when [minister John] Dawson took Caroline by the hand and led her down the shelving

bank into the limpid stream. They had attained about half
the desired depth, when she requested him to stop a moment,
and, turning to those on the bank, waving her hand, she
said, "Farewell, young friends! Farewell, Julia!" The effect
was electrical. The whole audience convulsed, and tears
rained down from eyes unused to weeping. ... Upon coming
up out of the water, Julia rushed forward to meet her friend,
embracing her, and crying out in agonizing tones, "Oh,
Carrie! You must not leave me! Mr. Dawson, pray for me.
Mr. Mallory, pray for me?"[1]

I was moved the first time I read that account, and I continue to be moved
because it properly illustrates that great division between the world and the
church. Here a young girl saw herself as leaving the friends she had in the
world for the companionship and the true fellowship of the local church.
She would now have a new set of friends. She would find her great joys
among that new set of friends. More than likely, she would spend her life
among them in this very community. As a believer she was now choosing to
live entirely differently than she had before, God giving her the grace to do
that. That is the proper picture, and that is what baptism helps us to see—it
is a visible way of seeing that tremendous difference, that great line between
the world and the church. We tend not to see it so deeply and meaningfully
as Carrie saw it when she was baptized so many years ago.

The Corinthian assembly was a body of believers that had begun to blur
the distinction between the world and the church. In 1 Corinthians 5, the
apostle Paul addresses several problems in the Corinthian church. It was a
problem-filled fellowship, not unlike some of the churches readers may be
part of. One of its problems had to do with this blending of the world and
the church by their attitude concerning an evil person among them.

I want to write out the entire text of 1 Corinthians 5; as you read
this short account, watch carefully for the sin the church was committing

---

1. Gregory A. Wills, *Democratic Religion in the South* (New York: Oxford University Press,
1997), 16.

and how it was violating the agreement between them. Then take note of the forceful way the apostle Paul tells the church to act in relation to this individual who has sinned. If you look for these things, you will feel the impact of this passage much better.

> It is actually reported that there is sexual immorality among you, and of a kind that is not tolerated even among pagans, for a man has his father's wife. And you are arrogant! Ought you not rather to mourn?
>
> Let him who has done this be removed from among you. For though absent in body, I am present in spirit; and as if present, I have already pronounced judgment on the one who did such a thing. When you are assembled in the name of the Lord Jesus and my spirit is present, with the power of our Lord Jesus, you are to deliver this man to Satan for the destruction of the flesh, so that his spirit may be saved in the day of the Lord.
>
> Your boasting is not good. Do you not know that a little leaven leavens the whole lump? Cleanse out the old leaven that you may be a new lump, as you really are unleavened. For Christ, our Passover lamb, has been sacrificed. Let us therefore celebrate the festival, not with the old leaven, the leaven of malice and evil, but with the unleavened bread of sincerity and truth.
>
> I wrote to you in my letter not to associate with sexually immoral people—not at all meaning the sexually immoral of this world, or the greedy and swindlers, or idolaters, since then you would need to go out of the world. But now I am writing to you not to associate with anyone who bears the name of brother if he is guilty of sexual immorality or greed, or is an idolater, reviler, drunkard, or swindler—not even to eat with such a one.
>
> For what have I to do with judging outsiders? Is it not those inside the church whom you are to judge? God judges

those outside. "Purge the evil person from among you."
(1 Cor 5:1–13 ESV)

You can feel the apostle's intense desire to keep the community pure. Now let us highlight five observations coming out of this text of Scripture that will help us to see the import of our relationship in the membership of a local church. If your church does not think in harmony on these things and act on them, you will forfeit the church's integrity before the believing and unbelieving world.

THE CHURCH IS A SOCIETY WITH RULES

The first observation is found in verses 1 and 2. Let me state that over again. "It is actually reported that there is sexual immorality among you, and of a kind that is not tolerated even among pagans, for a man has his father's wife. And you are arrogant! Ought you not rather to mourn?"

The observation I wish for us to see from these first two verses is very simply this: when you enter the church of the living God, you are joining a society with rules.

Obviously, the rule that is glaring at us right here is the command that underlies Paul's alarm: there will be no sexual immorality in the church. That is not the only rule, however. If you go on down in the text, you find that Paul says in verse 11: "But now I am writing to you not to associate with anyone who bears the name of brother if he is guilty of sexual immorality or greed, or is an idolater, reviler, drunkard, or swindler—not even to eat with such a one." There will be no extortion; there will be no idolatry; there will be no greed; there will be no drunkenness; there will be no reviling. There will be no deacon who reviles. There will be no Sunday school teacher who is covetous. There will be no member who is a drunkard on the sly. There are boundaries in the church.

Now, the apostle Paul is noticeably alarmed after hearing this report and writes what he writes with his mouth agape. He is trying to display to them that this is a very foolish and difficult place in which they find themselves in that they have condoned sexual immorality, and even beyond that a sexual immorality that is of a sort that even the gentiles condemn. In other words, even among the world, which is what the word "gentiles" really conveys, there is a measure of decorum and some conviction that this is wrong. Even in our day of an elasticized conscience, most of society, even the unbelieving society, would say that it is wrong for a man to have his father's wife in a sexual relationship. So, he is shocked! But the church, on the other hand, rather than being shocked and having a kinship with the apostle in his amazement, is tolerating it beautifully. If this were a news item in our day, the church would be leading the way advocating acceptance of the immoral man as a Christian virtue.

Paul believes that their failure to be shocked is arrogance. He says they are puffed up instead of mourning, indicating that they are in fact proud of their tolerance. We think in our day as well that such toleration is high in the hierarchy of spiritual virtues, and therefore a person surely is not Christian unless she is accepting of every kind of indiscretion. Some of us speak as if this were a new thing, but it is an old Corinthian problem.

It is also somewhat difficult for churches to realize that we have rules and we must abide by them, because somehow some of us think that such strictness mitigates against a good and correct concept of grace. In other words, here is a person who has come along having lived a sexually immoral life or having lived in the world and done any assortment of awful things, but he comes to Jesus Christ, and the Lord does not take his former life into account. He erases everything—he receives him by grace based on what Jesus Christ has done.

So, we mistakenly think the church must not have any rules or boundaries because if we came to Christ by grace and are fully accepted by grace, we must be accepted graciously by the church regardless of what we are currently doing. But that is not what this text teaches us. This text teaches us that when we come into the church, we come into a society with rules and boundaries.

I do not believe you are strict enough in your churches. Let me read something for you. Here are one congregation's rules about membership. I will not tell you the name of this congregation at first, and I am not saying

I espouse what it is doing or how it is saying it. But, I want to show you one congregation that at least has some strictness about what it means to be a member. It expresses this in its bylaws:

> Any member who does not have a registered attendance, identified financial support, definite service contribution, and/or expressed interest in loyalty within a six month's period, shall be notified by the Board of Directors in writing within 30 days prior to any congregational meeting that he or she has been placed on an inactive member list and is not eligible to vote at any meeting of the church.

Again, I am not saying this group has discovered the best way to deal with membership, the right way or the wrong way. I am only saying that here is a group that has some strictness about what it means to be a member.

Would you like to know who these people are? This bylaw comes from the Metropolitan Community Church of Los Angeles, the famous LGBT organization. Now what I am telling you is this: they are stricter than most of your churches. Chances are very good that if you had a homosexual or bisexual person in your congregation, your church would be puffed up and would tolerate what it found. At a minimum, your church would not know what to do, or if it did, would not have the will to do it. But this text teaches us that the local church is to have rules and we must abide by them.

THE CHURCH IS A SOCIETY THAT IS TO JUDGE ITS MEMBERS

The second observation is found in verses 3–5. I want you to read it again: "Let him who has done this be removed from among you. For though absent in body, I am present in spirit; and as if present, I have already pronounced judgment on the one who did such a thing." He continues, "When you are assembled in the name of the Lord Jesus and my spirit is present, with the power of our Lord Jesus, you are to deliver this man to Satan for the destruction of the flesh, so that his spirit may be saved in the day of the Lord."

The second observation, then, is: the church is a society that judges its members. In fact, that the very word "judge" is used here in the passage ought to forever dispel the concept that Christians never judge. It is true that Jesus says, "Judge not lest you be judged," but what he means, of course, is that we are not to have that kind of critical judgment that puts down another to elevate ourselves. But to judge the members of a covenant community is necessary for the church. In fact, if we had the time, we would go on and read 1 Corinthians 6. There we find a full explanation about how courts ought to be set up within the church to judge between brothers. There are several passages that speak to the judgment that is made by believers. Every church discipline situation is a judgment situation. The church is clearly a society that judges its members.

Now, the apostle Paul is very excited here. The commentator Hendrickson says that he takes the gavel in his hand, so to speak, and chairs the meeting of the local church even though he is absent.[2] He is so adamant about what he believes and so sure that this man ought to be judged that he says, in so many words, "Just think of me as being there, and I'll tell you ahead of time what my decision is. This man is to be expelled." Then he adds to that, "Not only as if I were there with my apostolic authority, but with the name or the authority of the Lord Jesus Christ as well!" In other words, he is sure where Jesus stands on this issue.

"Deliver this man to Satan." The delivering of one to Satan is another way of saying that they are to excommunicate the man from the church. To put it simply, here is a man professing to be a Christian and claiming to be under the headship of Christ by his membership, but in fact he is acting as a non-Christian. He is to be put away from the other members and put out into the world, where Satan is the authority. Satan, being a cruel taskmaster, will make it hard on his body, and hopefully he will be converted before the day of the Lord. As he remembers what the church was like, what he has heard from the church, and all those who loved him, perhaps he will yet be

---

2. Simon Kistemaker, "'Deliver this man to Satan' (1 Cor 5:5): A Case Study in Church Discipline." The Masters Seminary Journal 3,1 (Spring 1992): 37–38.

truly converted. I think that is the essence of what is being said. To review, the second observation is: the church is a society that judges its members.

THE CHURCH HAS GOOD REASON TO EXPECT ITS MEMBERS TO CONFORM TO THE RULES

I will give you the third observation before we read it: the church not only has rules and must judge its members, but the church also has good reason to expect members to conform to the rules. Let me provide verses 6–8:

> Your glorying is not good. Do you not know that a little leaven leavens the whole lump? Therefore, purge out the old leaven, that you may be a new lump, since you truly are unleavened. For indeed Christ, our Passover, was sacrificed for us. Therefore let us keep the feast, not with the old leaven, nor with the leaven of malice and wickedness, but with the unleavened bread of sincerity and truth.

Paul's example is that a little leaven leavens the whole lump of dough. He is saying, "You are the unleavened of God." In the Old Testament picture of the Passover, the Jews would take a period of days to clean up every speck of leaven from their houses before the festival. Leaven represented evil, and all the leaven, therefore, was to be removed. Then they were able to sacrifice the Passover lamb. To paraphrase, "Christ has been sacrificed, and you are therefore the unleavened as the church of God. That is who you are, but somehow you have added to yourselves this man who has done this evil, and it has caused some leaven or evil to enter the fellowship. You had better be careful to remove it. A little leaven leavens the whole lump of dough. Purge this leaven out from you."

Now, to those of you who cook, what would it be like if you left that chicken you were planning to cook on the counter for two weeks before using it? I have no idea where maggots come from, but I am sure that they would show up in that chicken. They would be there crawling in and out of the carcass right on your counter. The place would stink, and you would know you had a contaminated piece of meat. Now what if you took that contaminated piece of meat and you put it in a container with a fresh chicken? What would happen? Well, obviously, the fresh chicken would overwhelm the contamination of the rotten chicken, correct? No, it does not ever work that way, does it? Rather, the rotten chicken would contaminate the fresh chicken and would ruin it.

You see, somehow, we have gotten the idea that we should tolerate sin in our churches. That we should be so magnanimous that any kind of person may be allowed among our church people. We think, somehow, we will surely improve them. But the opposite is happening. I choose to believe that what the apostle Paul says here is true. Do you believe it? It is true that there are people who struggle with sin and want desperately to rid themselves of it. We should be glad to have people who are weak yet seeking help. But this unrepentant man presents another case.

We cannot just say it is true that evil people contaminate the rest, however, without corresponding action. If these evil persons among you are not lovingly but firmly dealt with, your supposed gracious spirit will be the ruin of some. A little leaven does leaven the whole lump of dough. So, if you have a Sunday school teacher who is getting drunk in private, or a greedy businessman who steals from his employer, or person who slanders others, or a gay person who teaches your youth, you are arrogant and foolish to permit this to continue. In Haggai 2:10–14 and Hebrews 12:14–16 the authors tell us that clearly. But I will leave that for you to read. Even if no other Scripture mentioned it, this passage would be enough. In fact, common sense itself ought to tell us that there is good reason to judge those who are consistently disobedient among us.

WHEN A CHURCH JUDGES ITS MEMBERS, IT REMOVES ITS MOST PRECIOUS GIFT—FELLOWSHIP

The fourth observation is found in verses 9–11. Paul says, "I wrote to you in my letter not to associate with sexually immoral people— not at all meaning the sexually immoral of this world, or the greedy and swindlers, or idolaters, since then you would need to go out of the world. But now I am writing to you not to associate with anyone who bears the name of brother if he is guilty of sexual immorality or greed, or is an idolater, reviler, drunkard, or swindler—not even to eat with such a one."

The point is this: ultimately, when a church judges its members, it withdraws its most precious gift—its fellowship. But, because our churches are so worldly and mixed, we have not really known the joys and the beauty of a spiritual community as it is supposed to be. We therefore think removing somebody from the church has very little potency. But if you have ever known the beauty of relationships with brothers and sisters in Christ and have tasted the sweetness of that kind of relationship as God intended it, it will almost destroy you to think of being removed from it.

When I think of my own propensity to sin and the foolish things that I could do, then think that I could stupidly go into gross sin, then lose fellowship with the people that I love the most in all this world, it is just too much for me to consider. Such a thought stops me in my tracks and makes me say I do not want to be that kind of man. I want to be careful about the way that I live.

Paul declares that the church is not even to eat with such a one. In fact, several very strong statements are made concerning him. Look at verse 2, "That he might be taken away from among you." And he says in verse 5, "Deliver this one over to Satan." Next, he urges in verse 7, "Cleanse out the old leaven." Then he reminds them in verse 11: "I have written to you not to associate with anyone" who lives like this. And at the end of verse 11 Paul exhorts, "Not even to eat with such a one." Then finally, when we get to the end of the chapter, verse 13, he charges them, "Purge the evil person from among you."

When you discipline a person who does not repent, you will finally come to that extreme place where the person is to be put out of the assembly. What do those words mean? Do they mean that the person should not be permitted to the Lord's Table? Yes, he is affirming that. The Lord's Supper is the greatest expression of our union with Christ and with each other. In fact, it is probably what is meant by the metaphor he uses in verse 8, "Therefore let us keep the feast, not with old leaven." He is saying, Do not let us come to the table of the Lord with the old leaven—the leaven of evil or maliciousness. Yes, it means that certainly.

It also means that we put him out from the membership of the church by taking him off the rolls so that he cannot contribute to the decision-making of the church or have the privilege of representing the church. It also means that he would not be given the appellation "Christian," or "brother" (see Matt 18:17–18).

Could it possibly mean as well that the person is not even allowed to join you in the meetings of the church? Yes. You see, the early church of Corinth and other early churches, it appears, ate a meal called the Lord's Supper every Lord's Day. We find this spelled out in 1 Corinthians 11. So, this restriction of being removed from the main meeting of the church when the communion meal was eaten is a major part of what it means not to eat with this person.

What is the most common occasion for that fellowship if it is not our gathering together under the ministry of the word and prayer? The sharing of the biblical "one anothers" and the Communion meal on the Lord's Day—what is this fellowship if it is not at least that? When you are meeting for the express purpose of worshiping God and having fellowship with believers, you must not allow the man who has been removed to enjoy that privilege. I know that the Bible mentions in 1 Corinthians 14 a nonbeliever wandering into the church and being convicted by the words spoken. But this is not the man who is expressly being forbidden this privilege. This language is strong indeed when it declares the person should be "taken away from among you," "expel[led]," or "put away from yourselves." The church is admonished, "Do not even associate with them" and "Do not even eat with them."

We have a meal in our church every Sunday when we gather together, but we are not even to eat with that person who has been expelled. Our fellowship is the most precious gift we must give our professing brothers and sisters. But, God says, we must withdraw from the erring one to keep the church pure and to do the best for the sinning person. You see, church discipline is not just for the individual. It hopes that the person under the cruel mastery of the devil might come to his senses and be saved for the day of the Lord. But, I believe it is mainly for the purity of the church. God intends for his church to be pure.

FAILURE TO PURGE THOSE WHO ARE WICKED AMONG YOU IS FLAGRANT DISOBEDIENCE

Here is the final observation, from verses 12 and 13. First read the passage: "For what have I to do with judging those also who are outside? Do you not judge those who are inside? But those who are outside God judges. Therefore, put away from yourselves the evil person." It can be observed: failure of the church to purge wicked people from among its membership is flagrant disobedience on the church's part.

In fact, to fail in this is a double disobedience and a double shame. On the one hand, it is the hosting of evil in your midst, which is wrong and dangerous. But the other shame is this; that the church is not obeying the clear command of God. That is the emphasis in this text. When Paul says, "Expel from yourselves that evil person," he quotes Old Testament passages from the book of Deuteronomy. The phrase shows up several times in the book of Deuteronomy. There it is mentioned in the singular. The subject "you," the implied "you" of the imperative (you put away, you expel), is in the singular in Deuteronomy. But the apostle Paul changes that to the plural and speaks to the whole church. He says "you together" purge away or expel this person from your midst. It is an obvious and plain command from the Lord himself. We cannot deny that God has commanded this, and failure on the part of the church to do this is clearly sin on the church's part.

REPENTANCE BY A LOCAL CHURCH

Our forebears disciplined a sizable number of people. This was true in most denominations. In the earliest days of the Baptist work in America in the early 1800s, there was a considerable amount of discipline. Gregory Wills states that in Georgia 3 to 4 percent of the Baptist people were brought to a church trial, and 1 to 2 percent had to be excommunicated on a yearly basis. These statistics we take to be somewhat representative of other parts of the country. They included discipline for nonattenders.[3]

Churches that come to their senses about their failure to be a church and to protect the preciousness of the relationship that they have together, who are therefore casually and even arrogantly tolerating sin, should be

---

3. Wills, *Democratic Religion in the South*.

on their faces in repentance when they see what God requires. The people should confess, "O God, we as a church have disobeyed you. We have taken lightly your command to protect the fellowship of the church. This is sin and dangerous neglect on our part." This is something for the church to repent of, and there is a lot of historical data about churches repenting of sin in the Scriptures.

You who are leaders have been entrusted with a body of professing saints. You are not permitted to gather them and then fail to watch over them. You have a command from God to maintain the soundness of the church's spiritual union. What will you do with that? We cannot blame others who have presented us with the problems for that which we are also passing on to the next generation. If we are to have a more biblical church, we must restore accountability. We are not just living with each other in the local body of Christ. No, we are in a spiritual familial union. In this sacred union on a high and spiritual level, we will experience our greatest joys—if that union remains pure. We have neglected our responsibilities for a long time in this arena, but our backlog of undone work is no excuse for delay.